WINNING
BY THE RULES

ETHICS AND SUCCESS IN THE INSURANCE PROFESSION

BY KEN BROWNLEE, CPCU

The
NATIONAL
UNDERWRITER
Company
PROFESSIONAL PUBLISHING GROUP

P.O. Box 14367 • Cincinnati, Ohio 45250-0367
1-800-543-0874 • www.nationalunderwriter.com

This publication is designed to provide accurate and authoritative information in regard to the subject matter covered. It is sold with the understanding that the publisher is not engaged in rendering legal, accounting or other professional service. If legal advice or other expert assistance is required, the services of a competent professional person should be sought. — From a Declaration of Principles jointly adopted by a Committee of the American Bar Association and a Committee of Publishers and Associations.

About the Author

Ken Brownlee has been involved with the insurance industry for nearly 35 years. During that time he was a multiline adjuster, corporate risk and claims manager, and course instructor for Crawford & Company. He earlier had been employed in journalism and social work. A graduate of Case-Western Reserve University in Cleveland, Ohio, Ken has Insurance Institute of America designations in claims, loss control, and risk management. He is a charter member of the claims section of the CPCU Society and founding editor of the *CPCU Claims Quarterly*. He also edited the *Crawford Risk Review*.

Active in insurance education and journalism for more than two decades, Ken has written many claims-related textbooks, including the three-volume *Casualty Insurance Claims, Fourth Edition,* and its companion handbook, *Casualty, Fire & Marine Investigation Checklists, Fifth Edition,* both coauthored with the late Patrick Magarick, LLM. Ken's latest book, the two-volume *Excess Liability: Rights and Duties of Commercial Risk Insureds and Insurers, Fourth Edition,* is a new edition of Magarick's *Excess Liability Third* and was coauthored with J. Robert Persons, J.D. These texts, published by the West Group, are updated frequently.

Ken contributed to *Essays on Ethics: Vol. II,* published in 1994 by The American College and the American Institute for CPCU. He also was a contributing author to *Insurance Operations, First Edition,* a CPCU 5 text. He has written for many insurance publications on a variety of subjects and has been a contributing editor to *Claims* magazine, a National Underwriter Company publication, for more than twenty years. He writes a monthly column entitled "The Claims-conscious Iconoclast" for *Claims*. He also speaks frequently at insurance-related seminars.

In addition to his writing and risk management consulting, Ken and his wife, Madonna, are active in church music in Atlanta, Georgia. He has taken a number of years of theological instruction and is a commissioned lay minister affiliated with Atlanta's Episcopal Cathedral of St. Philip. He also has written a mystery novel and a number of historical articles. He and his wife, a professional organist, travel extensively.

Winning by the Rules
Ethics and Success in the Insurance Profession

Table of Contents

Foreword

The concept of ethics has been discussed and debated since the time of Socrates. I clearly remember the first time I consciously argued the pros and cons of behavior. It was during a high school class discussion of the protagonist's actions in the classic, *Billy Budd*. The discussion taught me something very important—that ethical behavior can neither be legislated nor strictly defined by statute or legal ruling. In life and profession, this belief has served me well. And over time I have learned *how* to make ethical decisions and not look for guidelines to follow in every situation.

Elise M. Farnham, CPCU, AIM, ARM, CPIW, is vice president for Crawford & Company, a diversified risk management and insurance services firm with home offices in Atlanta, Georgia. Ms. Farnham is past national president of NAIW (1998-99) and a member of the Insurance Professionals of Atlanta. She also is treasurer of the Georgia Chapter of CPCU (2001) and a member of the society's 2001 Annual Meeting Task Force. She serves on the ARM advisory panel for the American Institute for CPCU and the educational advisory panel for *Claims* magazine's Annual Claims Expo (ACE).

We can find parallels in modern literature. For example, in *Harry Potter and the Chamber of Secrets*, society fares no better when attempting to legislate ethical behavior. J. K. Rowling has created the Office of Improper Use of Magic at the Ministry of Magic, but, still, wizards and magicians find themselves in situations not clearly defined by the rules and regulations.

When it comes to settling a claim, insurance professionals are no better off. Yet, consumers should feel confident in the ethical values of insurance professionals and trust that they will act in a highly ethical manner. After all, our product is a promise to pay (under specified circumstances), and consumers need to have confidence and trust that we will keep that promise. Along with this, we have a responsibility to be clear about what we are promising and how and when we will deliver on that promise.

Maintaining high ethical standards, even when the situation is not black and white, is the primary role of the insurance professional. There seem to be more and more gray areas today and more temptations as well. It is our duty and responsibility to make ethical decisions based on values of high integrity. Unfortunately, there is no laundry list of guidelines to help us in our decision-making process. Rather, through mentoring, ethics training, and publications such as this, we learn the process for recognizing unethical conduct and develop a decision-making process for ethical behavior.

On a different level, we all know that the decisions we make may have either a minimal impact or an impact so significant that it will change our lives. Either way, ethical decision-making processes should dictate the outcome.

We all feel disappointment upon learning of unethical activities among colleagues. And, each of us has bristled to learn of the need for prosecution of an employee who embezzled funds. Finally, many of us, at some point in our careers, have been forced to terminate business relationships with unethical vendors, carriers, and risks. These decisions were not easy, and each contained at least some downside risk.

In each case, it was imperative that executive management fully supported our actions. In fact for strong ethics to be our hallmark, executive management must not only set the standard and support the decisions of their employees, they must foster a corporate culture that encourages ethical decision-making.

A great example is The Insurance Women of Dallas, whose members must fulfill requirements to earn the designation of Certified Professional Insurance Woman (CPIW) from the National Association of Insurance Women (International). The outward sign of completing this coursework is a plaque containing the CPIW's Code of Ethics. I proudly display such a plaque in my office. To me, it is not only a reminder of my code of ethics, but I hope that it is a clear message that my beliefs and practices are centered in ethical behavior.

Behavioral scientists agree that values, which later become ethical practices, are typically developed during the early, formative years. I personally believe, however, that we can learn to make ethical decisions based on values such as integrity, honesty, and trust . . . particularly when we have an ethical corporate culture that supports our beliefs.

I hope that you, the insurance professional, will find this publication helpful in facing dilemmas that no doubt will arise in the industry's increasingly complex environment. We owe a debt to our industry for fostering ethics in all practices. Since we are ultimately "where the rubber meets the road," it is up to us to exercise good judgement in every decision we make—no matter how large or how small.

I believe that the meaning of ethics and the implications of ethical decision-making shared in this book will serve our profession well.

Dr. Lawrence Brandon, Chairman of the American Institutes for CPCU, probably stated it best in a speech to the Georgia Chapter of CPCU. He said, "We have only two things of importance in this business—our relationships and our reputations. Relationships are based on honesty and trust. Reputations are based on the integrity with which we do our work."

As headmaster, Professor Dumbledore said to Harry Potter at the conclusion of *Chamber of Secrets,* "It is our choices, Harry, that show what we truly are, far more than our abilities."

So it is for the insurance professional.

Elise M. Farnham, CPCU, AIM, ARM, CPIW

Introduction

The Context

"*Ethics has to do with duty—duty to self and/or duty to others. It is primarily individual or personal even when it relates to obligations and duties to others. The quality of human life has to do with both solitude and sociability. We do right or wrong by ourselves in that part of our lives lived inwardly or introvertedly and also in that part of our lives where we are reading and responding to other persons. This duality of individual and social morality is implicit in the very concept of ethics.*"

Dr. John C. Merrill
The Imperative of Freedom
(Hastings House 1974)

Dozens of definitions can be found for the word *ethics*. Most have to do with factors such as moral behavior, trust, beliefs and practices, attitudes, even right and wrong. Academically, ethics is a field of philosophy, as is logic. In one sense it is related to mathematics. An *integer* is a whole number; it has the same Latin root as the word *integrity*, which means wholeness. Ethics implies integrity or oneness. Two and two should equal four—if we try to make it equal five, the logical system has lost its integrity. Unethical behavior sometimes tries to make two and two equal five, and that creates problems.

The subject of ethics also is close to the field of religion, for religions often impose systems that imply ethical attitudes, practices, and behavior. However, the *Golden Rule* is not unique to the Judeo-Christian-Islamic faiths. Often those who are the least religious are the most ethical.

Words are important in understanding ethics. As Karen B. Veiger, CPCU, a member of the CPCU Society Ethics Committee, wrote in the November 2000 issue of *CPCU News* (Vol. 48, No. 8, p. 16):

> Are ethical decisions situational or absolute? More importantly, does it matter? These are questions that have generated philosophical debate for millennia. And despite their efforts, even our greatest thinkers—eastern and western, ancient and modern—have failed to answer them definitively. There may be no definitive answers. Nevertheless, the study of business ethics attempts to answer these questions in the context of organizational behavior.

Situational. Absolute. Words applied to ethics that raise issues for the ages. Aristotle may have been speaking of situational ethics when he defined ethics as conflicts in morality. Human endeavors often involve choices, a selection from several options. The options may all be good, or they may all be bad. The task is to select the ethical best to fit the situation. Absolutes often present problems: "Always speak the truth!" might be considered an absolute ethic. But what is truth? Those who appeal to courts of law to demonstrate the truth often find that it is not what they think it should be. It is not an absolute.

This book explores concepts of ethical behavior as they relate to the risk-spreading mechanism of insurance. It also discusses how insurance relates to the twenty-first century concept of enterprise risk management and the convergence of financial services such as banking, insurance, and securities. We then review how mistakes—whether we call them malpractice or errors and omissions—create professional liability exposures for the insurance practitioner. Such practitioners may be underwriters; agents or brokers; or adjusters, claim attorneys, and other claim representatives. Each has a different role in the overall insurance mechanism, yet each owes an ethical duty to the insured policyholder. The book then moves on to discuss how insurance ethics differ from and overlap with other areas of business ethics. We consider the standard rule of the marketplace: Buy Low, Sell High.

Many ideas in this book are derived from more than thirty-three years of experience in the claims and risk management arena, as well as work as a columnist and contributing editor for *Claims Magazine* (a National Underwriter Co. publication) under the name of *The Claims-Conscious Iconoclast*. That name has significance: an iconoclast is one who breaks images. Those images have to do with how claims adjusters view their vocation. Most of the issues apply equally to underwriters and agents or brokers.

Many insurance practitioners see themselves as part of a profession and act accordingly—seeking graduate-level education, becoming part of local or national professional organizations, and subscribing to a personal code of professional ethics. They are skilled practitioners who exude altruistic behavior, which is part of their integrity, their oneness, both at home and in business.

Unfortunately this is not the case with all adjusters, attorneys, claim representatives, agents, brokers, and underwriters. Often it also is not the case with insurance companies. In 1989 I, as the Iconoclast, suggested that the philosophy of Ebenezer Scrooge, made famous in Charles Dickens's *A Christmas Carol,* was not much different from the business philosophy that society was encountering in the late twentieth century. In many ways old Ebenezer was a very ethical man— hard working, thrifty, concerned with the welfare of his business. The twenty-first century global economy often seems to have as little room for concern about the Bob Cratchits of the world as did Scrooge. This is one of the reasons that society has acted through its governments to impose labor laws and establish agencies such as OSHA and the EEOC.

However, some aspects of American society have exhibited a great deal of concern with business ethics in recent decades. Vocal consumer advocates such as Ralph Nader have warned about the effects of industry on the environment, about unsafe products— including medications—and about shoddy workmanship. How many believe television ads boasting that one product is better than another? How many truly believe political promises? How many are cynical about the constant ups and downs in the stock markets, which often react solely on quarterly earnings reports? How many businesses have boomed and then busted because of unsustainable exuberance?

Is cutting qualified staff, education, research, and product development just to please the stock market the right thing to do? This question cannot be answered without also considering that the stock market now includes millions of families and retirees who depend upon it for retirement survival, as well as an insurance industry that relies upon investments to provide coverage at reasonable rates. As Aristotle suggests, there are conflicts in morality, including the morality of the marketplace.

It has only been in the last decade or two that business and law schools have included ethics courses in their graduate degree requirements. Medical ethics also is a relatively new term, brought about through advances in medicine that often lead to very real and serious ethical dilemmas. Even ethical issues among the clergy have claimed national attention. Perhaps such interest is not new, but it seems to be of increasing concern to the current generations. Business can no longer be conducted on a handshake. People seem to look for ulterior motives in every offer and insist that their lawyers check the details of every contract. We live in an age of concern about ethics.

Among such concerns are those related to insurance. Various types of insurance no longer are relegated to corporations or the wealthy. We cannot purchase a home without property insurance to protect the collateral, borrow money without insurance on its repayment after death or disability, drive a car without mandated auto liability insurance, or get a car loan without physical damage insurance. Individuals without medical insurance are among a minority that has drawn national attention. Bids on governmental contracts require surety bonds, and bail bonds are required to get out of jail. Insurance is involved in all facets of life.

How can we know whether we have been sold the right insurance product at the right price? How can we know that our claims will be handled quickly, fairly, and with our best interests in mind? How can we know that the insurer we place coverage with will be there when needed? All of these are ethical issues.

Insurance may be termed peace of mind, a contract to alleviate concerns. This book addresses the vitally important issues that cannot be ignored when insurance is provided in a less than ethical manner. It also addresses the consequences of mistakes and breaches of ethical duty.

How will ethics be defined in the twenty-first century? Will the attitudes and beliefs of the past continue, or will the new economy usher in new ethics for a world in which communication is instant and business international? As each topic is explored chapter by chapter we add situational thought provokers for the reader's consideration. Hopefully these will prompt readers to delve further into the subject.

Insurance ethics involves a lot of words. By coincidence, many of those words begin with the letter *I*. The word *integrity* already has been explored. Other *I*-words are encountered throughout our survey of insurance ethics:

Information. Complete and accurate information lies at the heart of every aspect of insurance. All data must be precise if rating, underwriting, and claim settlements are to be equitable. Wrong or incomplete information leads to errors and therefore becomes unethical.

Imagination. Many may question what imagination has to do with ethics. It has a whole lot to do with it, from the marketing of insurance to the settlement of claims. The agent or broker must use his imagination to envision the various exposures an insurance applicant may encounter and to find the appropriate treatment for those exposures. The risk manager must be imaginative when ferreting out hazards. The underwriter must use imagination to envision what the risk she sees on paper truly represents. The claim representative must imagine himself as the damaged party in order to recognize various aspects of the loss and to envision which ones fall within the limits of the policy. True empathy requires imagination.

Initiative. The insurance specialist cannot simply be a fill-in-the-blanks and pull-the-handle type of employee. She must take the initiative to complete the task at hand and the responsibility for a correct outcome. That requires ingenuity, intelligence, imagination, and fortitude.

Individualism. Insurance is an industry based on the law of large numbers. However, to achieve the best ethical position it must treat each insured, each exposure, and each claim individually and with personal attention.

Indemnification. Insurance is often defined in terms of *indemnity*. That word even appears in the names of many insurance companies. It implies making whole, placing a party in the same position he was in prior to a loss. In reality, indemnification often is impossible to achieve. There can be no true indemnity when people are killed or suffer permanent injuries. Insurers, however, must strive for this objective as it is translated into monetary terms. Priceless is not an insurance term; all things must be valued monetarily. Sentiment, fame, and uniqueness are not normally insurable. The ethical aspect of indemnity is that, when indemnification is necessary, it must be achieved correctly. When a claim is either overpaid or underpaid, the loss has not been indemnified. Indemnification, therefore, is a very narrow line from which any deliberate straying can constitute unethical behavior.

Despite this, there are exceptions on both sides of the line. Policies with deductibles, coinsurance clauses, and similar limitations intentionally do not fully indemnify. On the other side, policies that provide replacement cost instead of actual cash value may exceed what legally is considered indemnification.

Chapter 1

The Historical Aspects

"Marcus Cato engaged in that most disreputable form of speculation, the underwriting of ships!"

Plutarch *(120-46 B.C.E.)*

The relationship of ethics to insurance is impossible to under stand without first understanding the principles and history of insurance as it relates to society. Insurance has always been and remains much different from almost any other type of business.

While some of the basics of business ethics apply equally to insurance, the ethical standard for insurance is much higher than that of business in general, where the watchword is *caveat emptor*—let the buyer beware. Society's rulers and regulators—legislative and judicial—have traditionally put the shoe on the other foot: let the *insurer* beware! It is with that *caveat* that insurance ethics finds support, if not a foundation.

It is necessary to understand the language of risk and insurance to fully understand insurance ethics. While most of the terms used in insurance are common, ordinary words, they take on significant meaning in the insurance context.

Risk. This word can have several meanings. It is a chance of loss. In some settings risk also can mean the exposure or subject of insurance, the person or object at risk. Risk is a crucial factor in insurance ethics because it lies at the root of what separates actuarially sound insurance from speculation or gambling.

Hazards. This word also has several meanings. In insurance jargon, a hazard generally is a condition or situation that makes it more likely for an occurrence, accident, or loss to happen. It also has other meanings that relate to specific perils. For example, some policies temporarily void coverage for loss when the hazard is increased beyond that which was anticipated. Hazards usually are considered to fall into one of three categories: physical, moral, and morale. Each has ethical implications.

Loss. Many insurance people use loss and claim interchangeably, but they are two very different concepts. A loss is an event—an occurrence, accident, or situation—that has life to it. That life begins with the hazards or circumstances that build until something (an insured peril or otherwise) occurs. But it does not stop there. Unless there is intervention, the situation grows worse and becomes more disruptive, expensive, and complicated. Something or someone must intervene to deal with the loss. It is a dynamic process.

Claim. A claim is simply a financial demand. While claims may involve more than just a demand for payment, most do not deal with all aspects of loss. Most involve only the direct or the indirect costs of loss, depending on what is covered by the policy. These costs may include aspects such as assisting the insured evaluate the loss (appraisal) or defending the insured in a court of law.

Exposure. This word also has several meanings. In some cases the words risk and exposure may be interchangeable. ("The insured *risk* is located at....". "The *exposure* is a frame structure located at ... .") Hazards often increase the exposure to loss; hence, in risk management terms if not insurance jargon, exposure represents the potential for loss. It often is expressed in monetary terms. ("Our exposure, should a loss occur, could be $2 million.") It also may refer to the limits of liability under a policy.

Peril. A peril is a cause of loss. It must be specific, and it often is defined in legal terms, either by the policy or the courts. A fire insurance policy, for example, rarely defines the word fire, but the peril is interpreted to mean only hostile fire and not friendly fire. Windstorm also may not be defined. However, if a breeze accidentally blows away a stack of $20 bills that a person is counting outdoors, it is unlikely that the insurer will consider it a covered windstorm loss. Perils can cause both direct and indirect loss, depending on the terms of the insurance contract.

Insurance. An insurance policy is simply a contractual means of transferring the risk of loss from one party to another for a fee. Insurance is simply a mechanism for spreading risks among a large number of homogeneous exposure units—regardless of whether those units are people, automobiles, buildings, or products. Certain characteristics of insurance must be taken into consideration if the transfer is to be an ethical one.

First, the risk must be *calculable.* War is generally considered an uninsurable peril (except in some specific policies) because the potential loss from a war is incalculable. The exposure is too great, and there is no prior loss history on which an actuarially sound rate can be established.

Next, insurance is said to be an *aleatory* contract, coming from the root word *aleatorius,* which means gambling. Insurance is uneven. One can pay $1 for one pound of potatoes, an even swap. But in insurance a policyholder may pay a premium and collect nothing— except a promise—if no loss occurs. A promise to pay has been purchased. On the other hand, if a loss does occur, the policyholder may collect many times the amount of the premium.

But insurance is not considered gambling. Using insurance for gambling purposes was outlawed in England in 1906 under the Marine Insurance Act. Nevertheless, the fact that insurance policies have been written on some unusual risks may give the appearance of gambling— risks such as hole-in-one golf tournament coverage, awards for finding the Loch Ness monster, and potential injury to a musician's fingers.

Insurance also is considered a *contract of adhesion.* With the exception of manuscript policies, in which the terms are negotiated between the insurance company and the policyholder, the insured must accept the contract as prepared by the insurer on virtually a take it or leave it, all or nothing, basis.

Insurance contracts also are said to be *unilateral.* After the premium has been paid, only the insurer is obliged to act in the event of a loss. This is not entirely true, however, because insurance contracts are also *conditional* contracts. Duties are imposed on both parties in the event of loss. Ethical issues often arise in the interpretation of some of these conditions.

Many insurers and underwriters have encountered financial difficulty by failing to remember that perils must meet certain criteria in order to be insurable. One criterion is that a large number of homogeneous exposure units must be subject to the peril. They also must be subject to both *definite* and *definitive loss.* The potential loss also must be, to quote Robert Mehr and Emerson Cammack in *Principles of Insurance* (Irwin Press 1972) "so large that the insured could not bear it himself without economic distress." Yet an insurable peril also must be economically feasible, and the likelihood of loss must be *calculable*, which means it is unlikely that massive loss will occur to many of the units at the same time.

Finally, to be insurable the loss must be *fortuitous* or totally accidental and unplanned, even though the possibility of the loss—but not the actual loss—may have been foreseen. There cannot be *adverse selection*, where only those who have a high risk of loss from a particular peril purchase coverage for it.

Absent these rules, insurance is little more than gambling, and insurers get into trouble when they forget them. Failure to adhere to them also poses serious ethical issues.

Ancient Societies and the Need for Protection

Since the days when families gathered together around a fire in a cave and used rocks, clubs, and sticks for protection and hunting, people have had to deal with risk. They built walls around their villages to keep out enemies and disease. They established systems of government and raised armies for defense. They formed allegiances with other villages for mutual aid. Eventually they designed systems to spread risks among those who shared them.

There is a legend that the concept of spreading risk began with Chinese farmers who were exposed to perils of river travel when shipping their goods to market. In what was probably a scheme dreamed up by some farmer's wife who was tired of the all or nothing risks of marketing, the farmers divided their loads among all the vessels that were traveling the river. They knew that some still would be lost, but most of each farmer's goods would reach the market.

Various types of marine insurance also were common in the Greek and Roman eras. The Phoenicians had what were called bottomry contracts on their ships, through which underwriters agreed to pay the owners a set amount should a ship or its cargo be lost at sea. Travel has always been difficult, and some of the ways to handle such risks remain from ancient times.

Ethical standards had a vital role in ancient rules and regulations. The professions swore to codes of ethics just as they do today. The Oath of Hippocrates is as relevant today as it was 2,500 years ago, and the graduating physician is just as obligated to obey it. Certain tenets, such as the clause, "To please no one will I prescribe a deadly drug…"

today generate considerable debate in medical ethics. The oath also requires the physician to "keep myself far from all intentional ill-doing and all seduction." When we consider the ethical issues surrounding assisted suicide, prescribing of unneeded medications, and other issues affecting the practice of medicine, it is easy to see how close the issue of ethics and codified oaths become.

The *Code of Laws of Hammurabi, King of Babylonia* specified that "if a builder builds a house . . . and does not make its construction meet the requirements and a wall falls in, that builder shall strengthen the wall at his own expense." This is not much different from the laws concerning products and completed operations today.

The foundations of much of our tort laws and insurance mechanisms are found in ancient texts, including Torah. The rules and regulations outlined in Exodus, for example, could describe modern legal procedures with only a few changes of words: auto for ox, or employee for servant. The laws provided for payments for damaged or destroyed property. There was also the early concept of indemnity in the rule of "eye for eye, tooth for tooth," an improvement over the blood feuds between families and tribes that could lead to war and destruction. Individuals no longer could legally take a life in exchange for a tooth.

Some laws and rules often do seem absolute and unchangeable. However, the idea that laws are inflexible can raise problems. As a wise insurance professor, Patrick Magarick, L.L.M., once warned, there are no absolutes. "Should an abused child," Magarick asked, "be required to 'honor' his mother and father?" Therein lies the ethical dilemma. Ethics, as Aristotle suggested, truly do involve conflicts in morality.

Insurance as Risk Management in Previous Centuries

While the insurance industry seems quite modern, it is actually a very old and honored institution. Guilds of insurance underwriters operated throughout the Middle Ages, usually in port cities with maritime risks. Marine policies were issued on ships out of Genoa, Italy, in 1347, and in 1468 the Grand Council of Venice established laws to govern the conduct of marine insurance.

Many earlier contracts resembled suretyship more than insurance, and an element of gambling often accompanied such underwriting.

One type of contract, called a *respondentia*, involved payment of a fee in addition to interest on loans made for cargoes. It was intended to compensate the lender for insuring the safety of the voyage. The contracts were risky, however, and in Greece funds held in trust for orphans could not be invested in such contracts.

Lombardian merchants operated many of the guilds. They traveled Europe bringing the Renaissance and enlightenment to its major cities. Many of them settled around the docks in London, and in the mid-1600s the second coffeehouse operated by Edward Loyd was located on Lombard Street. Loyd (the second *l* in his name was not added until the 1700s) was not in the insurance business. He was a coffee merchant, but he catered to businessmen who did accept risks for a fee. In this system, a businessman with a cargo to ship, a sea captain with a vessel for hire, or a ship owner seeking protection for a voyage, would approach the men seated in Edward Loyd's coffeehouse and discuss their risk—the cargo or the ship. If the prospective insured, or a broker he might have hired, convinced the person in the booth that the cargo had value and the ship was seaworthy, that businessman would agree to accept a percentage of the risk. He would write this percentage on the proposal and sign his name underneath. He was said to have *under written* that percentage of the risk. The merchant, sea captain, owner, or broker then would go to other booths to fill the slip. More than 300 years later worldwide risks are brokered and underwritten in the same manner by Underwriters at Lloyd's, London.

Edward Loyd did more than sell coffee. He quickly realized that the key to accurate and safe underwriting was information. He began to publish a listing of ships, *Lloyd's News*, which even today in its modern format is considered a necessity in marine underwriting. Through this regular publication the underwriters obtained information about who built a vessel, its captain and his reputation, the crew, and the ship's capabilities.

The underwriters took the risk of loss seriously, as each *name*— a syndicate member authorized to invest and underwrite at Lloyd's— was held to unlimited liability. A member had to pay each and every legitimate claim in full, even if it took his—or her (female monarchs being names, at least at one time)—last penny. It was this unlimited liability and Lloyd's reputation of paying claims in full that gave it a reputation as the world's most ethical insurer. It was not until the late twentieth century, when many Americans invested in Lloyd's syndicates—and then lost money when they were held to the unlimited liability on risks their partner underwriters accepted—that limits were placed upon such liability.

But the Underwriters at Lloyd's were responsible for much more than insuring ships. Lloyd's was a leader in devising loss control methods as well. Lloyd's was instrumental in the construction of lighthouse stations around the British coastline and in the development of the lifeboat.

By the twentieth century the insurance industry was a leader in the fight to reduce losses. From early lifesaving procedures to today's independent testing of products and vehicles and the issuing of fire codes, the insurance industry has endorsed loss engineering as a vital part of its responsibility to both investors and policyholders. In some coverages, such as boiler and machinery insurance, much of the premium is designated for regular inspections and accident prevention. Even today marine policies are not written until a marine surveyor has inspected the vessel.

The concept of honesty and high ethical standards was inherent throughout the history of insurance. To illustrate, in 1659 one London marine underwriter, Samuel Pepys, was offered 15 percent on a ship that was reported late while under way to Newcastle. Late ships were not uncommon in sailing days when the winds might not conform with a sea captain's desires, but this did not always mean that the ship was lost. Pepys received information from the Royal Admiralty that the ship might already be safe in a harbor, and he could have profited by concealing this fact. As a man of integrity, he would not do so.

A little over 200 years later a similar situation arose in the overdue market when, at closing time in London on April 15, 1912, word reached London brokers that the White Star Line's *Titanic* had struck an iceberg. That was all that was known, and the brokers at the Bowring brokerage firm

Do You Agree?

The concept of honesty and high ethical standards was inherent throughout the history of insurance.

were asked to purchase overdue reinsurance at the best possible rate. A young broker was dispatched to the old Lloyd's in the Royal Exchange to see what could be done.

As Godfrey Hodgson tells the story in *Lloyd's of London*, (Viking Press 1984):

> . . .after searching the [Underwriting] Room, the Captain's Room and elsewhere with no results, on the stairway … he met John Povah, a well-respected leader in the overdue market. On being offered the risk, Povah remarked, "The rate at the moment is 25 guineas per cent, but if you want me to write so large an amount as that, I must have 30 guineas." Having an order for the "best possible" on a total loss basis, the offer was accepted, and Povah said, "Bring the slip round to me tomorrow and I will put it down—I am in a hurry now."

By the following morning it was certain that the *Titanic* was a total loss. Continues Hodgson, "There was likewise no doubt in anyone's mind that the verbal acceptance was binding." The Underwriters paid out more than £1,400,000 in claims on the famous unsinkable ship.

Early Life Insurance

Life insurance was developed in London during the sixteenth century, but its beginnings were often as much a matter of gambling as actuarially sound insurance. In London's Old Drury Ale House on June 18, 1536, a group of underwriters got the idea of insuring the life of one of their fellow companions, William Gybbons. They considered him to be a "hail fellow well met . . . healthy of person, and apparently destined to live the full Biblical 'three score and ten.'" Underwriter Richard Martin and his partners agreed to insure the life of Gybbons for approximately £500 at a rate of .04 percent for twelve months and the contract was drawn. Unfortunately, William Gybbons died on May 29, 1537.

When Mrs. Gybbons tried to collect, the underwriters denied her claim, alleging that she misunderstood—they had meant twelve *lunar* months—and the coverage had lapsed on May 20, nine days before her husband's death. The feisty Widow Gybbons sued Martin and the other underwriters for breach of contract. In a ruling that still has application in the twenty-first century, the court found that any ambiguity in an insurance policy written by the insurers—the contract of adhesion theory of insurance—should be interpreted in favor of the insured.

Eighteenth Century American Insurance Endeavors

Information has been the key to the insurance industry in America as well as internationally. Accurate information reported promptly and correctly lies at the root of insurance ethics. Underwriters cannot do their jobs without complete and correct details about the risk; loss engineers cannot help to prevent losses without extensive information about previous losses; agents and brokers cannot properly place the risk without understanding it.

In the history of the Philadelphia Contributionship for the Insurance of Houses from Loss by Fire, an insurance company founded by Benjamin Franklin in 1752, Nicholas B. Wainwright writes in *A Philadelphia Story* (published by the insurer in 1952):

> A great fire hazard of the times [the 1750s] was the cleaning and repairing of ship bottoms at the wharves, which required the heating of pitch. Since liability for breaming vessels, as it was called, was unacceptable to the Directors (of the Philadelphia Contributionship) Franklin was ordered to publish an advertisement in his *Gazette* notifying the contributors [the mutual insureds] that storing of gunpowder in town and breaming ships at wharves are 'contrary to law and that if any member of this Society receives any damage thereby occasioned by himself it shall be deemed prejudicial to this insurance.' Several years later, in 1756, during the French and Indian War, it was agreed to advertise in the *Gazette* a reward of £15 to anyone who shall give warning to the Company of any quantity of gun powder concealed in any store or house, contrary to a law of the province now in force, so that the offender may be legally convicted.

The insurers obviously were interested in preventing losses that would affect not only their mutual interests as the insurer, but also the interests of their insureds, individually and corporately.

Fire insurance was popular in American cities well before the Revolutionary War. Most buildings of the era were built of wood, and fires were common. London had burned to the ground in 1666, a loss that led to Dr. Nicholas Barbon founding the first British fire insurance company. American cities also were vulnerable to total destruction by fire.

In the eighteenth and early nineteenth centuries, the fire insurers normally operated the fire departments with their horse-drawn water pumps, hoses, and buckets. The outward symbol of insurance was a *fire mark*, a plaque that was placed high on a house to show that it was insured. The fire department attacked fires in homes or buildings bearing a mark but departed if it were missing, suggesting to the owners that they ought to insure their next structure. Fire marks were used by insurance companies throughout the world, and even today the Philadelphia Contributionship provides fire marks to its insureds.

Nineteenth Century Insurance Crises

The peril of fire, along with disease epidemics, plagued America during the 1800s. As the nation expanded westward, diseases such as smallpox ravaged thousands of immigrants who dug the canals and laid the tracks of the new steam railways. America's life insurance industry was still in its infancy, although marine underwriters had written life policies and annuities since 1721. Many of the early life insurers were affiliated with religious organizations, and it was often the religious and fraternal organizations that provided aid to distressed widows and orphans.

As canals were completed and rail lines connected, the builders and thousands of immigrant workers settled into growing cities like Chicago, St. Louis, Cleveland, Detroit, and Cincinnati. Many frame buildings in the East had been replaced with stone and brick after major fires, but cities of the West (as the Midwest then was considered) were largely comprised of wooden structures. Insurance companies were started in order to provide protection. However, these companies soon learned an important lesson as vital today as then: they had to spread the risk. In May of 1849, a dock fire in St. Louis destroyed twenty-seven Mississippi River steamboats before spreading to the downtown area and destroying it, too. Insurers that had written policies on a number of the steamboats or buildings suffered major losses. But many paid their claims and survived.

On the evening of October 8, 1871, a Chicago neighbor of an Irish immigrant, Mrs. Jeremiah O'Leary, needed some milk. She returned to her barn where, according to early statements obtained by adjusters, her cow kicked over a lantern and started a fire. A watchman in the city hall fire tower was entertaining his girlfriend and did not immediately notice the smoke. When he did, he reported an incorrect location. An alarm box near the fire also malfunctioned, so the fire department was delayed in reaching the fire on Chicago's west side. The conflagration that followed destroyed 1,687 acres of Chicago.

Of the estimated $190.5 million loss, more than $100 million was insured by 202 different fire insurance companies. Of these, sixty-eight paid claims until they went broke, eighty-three partially paid their claims, and fifty-one paid in full. A similar situation occurred when fire destroyed San Francisco after the April 18, 1906, earthquake. Of 108 insurance companies involved in the $225 million loss, only eighteen paid less than 75 percent of their claims, and twenty-seven insurers paid in full.

Casualty coverages were slower to develop. While the roots of workers compensation may have appeared in the Bible, the concept of a no fault system involving insurance first emerged in Germany during the latter 1800s, perhaps under some of the same social influences that led to the writings of Karl Marx. The first attempt at a workers compensation law in the United States was in 1902, when Maryland passed a bill that was promptly declared unconstitutional. New York legislation in 1910 was more successful, and a workers compensation policy was first issued in 1911.

> **A Little Bit of History**
>
> *The great Chicago fire of 1871 destroyed 1,687 acres of the city. Of the estimated $190.5 million loss, more than $100 million was insured by 202 different fire insurance companies.*

Previously America and Canada had followed the traditional common law theories of English law, with a few exceptions. Common law is basically case law, in which earlier court decisions establish legal doctrines and principles. Negligence rules were considerably less liberal than in the twenty-first century. A claim died with the victim, regardless of the amount of liability or the loss to the victim's family. Contributory negligence of any slight amount was a total defense to a claim against a tortfeasor. In employment, it was often the injured worker who contributed in some way to his or her own injury, and she could be barred from any recovery against the employer.

Early third-party liability policies did exist, but they were written primarily on an *indemnification* basis. An insured who was sued had to defend himself. If a court awarded damages, the policyholder had to pay them. Only then could he seek reimbursement from the insurer. The concept of pay on behalf of the insured came later.

Liability coverage that was written in the 1890s was limited in scope. The Travelers issued the first automobile liability policy to a Buffalo physician, Dr. Truman J. Martin, on February 1, 1898. It was based on a teamsters' liability form. Products liability coverage was first marketed in 1910.

Changing Attitudes in the Twentieth Century

The insurance industry is constantly evolving. Both industry and policyholder attitudes have evolved, and the general public's perception of the industry—especially of the industry's ethics—also fluctuates. Half the public relations battle has been won when the public believes it can trust its insurers. On the other hand, when the news media reports stories of mishandled and disputed claims and the use of investigative services that are questionable, the public relations battle has been lost for the entire insurance industry.

The late Pat Magarick, L.L.M., author of a number of insurance claim textbooks and longtime columnist for National Underwriter Company's *Claims Magazine*, described his claims department service during the Depression years of the 1930s. He worked for "a local cut-rate insurance company with more than a dozen adjusters, most of whom were recruited from sales and blue collar positions and given basic training on the job.... The motto of this [unnamed and now defunct] company was 'get a release as soon as possible and pay as little as possible for it.' Every morning we were given fifty single dollar bills and instructed to count them out one at a time when making an offer of settlement."

Every dollar mattered—to the insured, claimant, and insurance company. It was the ethic of the marketplace: buy low, sell high. When the insurer "buys" a settlement, it does so at the least possible cost. When it sells its policies, it should sell at a price that will cover company operations and claim settlements. Both are subject to negotiation. There is nothing unethical about negotiating settlements and premiums. What is unethical is to put the insurance product, which is really only the peace of mind discussed earlier and the settlement of claims, on a take it or leave it basis. Insurance claims do not, and ought not, come with bar codes like food in a grocery store. Each claim, each insured or claimant, each factor of damages or injuries, is different. Claims cannot be handled with a one size fits all mentality. Unfortunately, that is often the way the public views the industry.

Do You agree?

There is nothing unethical about negotiating settlements and premiums. What is unethical is to put the insurance product, which is really only peace of mind and the settlement of claims, on a take it or leave it basis. Claims cannot be handled with a one size fits all mentality.

If an insurer settles its claims at too high a price, it is breaching that marketplace ethic as much as if it sells its product, the policy, at too low a price. The careful balance of both paying and charging the right amounts to remain solvent and be fair is crucial.

Following the resurgence of the nation's growth after World War II, insurers were able to hire many former GIs as claim adjusters. Many of them had taken advantage of the GI Bill to obtain college and law degrees. The economy was strong, and insurers profited from their investments. The industry enjoyed positive growth and favorable public attitudes. Most families had at least one automobile, and many had new homes, all of which required insurance. The suburbs were absorbing the overflow from cities, and men with steady employment could take their families on vacations. Despite the Cold War, there was a sense of optimism.

Insurers formerly dealt in one type of coverage—life, health, property, surety, or liability. Then package policies were introduced to offer first-party property and medical coverage along with liability coverage. Instead of having separate policies, a homeowner could get all three types of coverage in a single form from a single insurer. Auto insurers could sell medical payments, liability, and physical damage coverage in the same policy. These conveniences helped to improve public attitudes toward insurers.

Surveys taken during that era showed that most Americans held favorable attitudes toward insurance companies. Approval rates topped 68 percent, and most policyholders rated their own insurers higher than the other guy's.

Much of this was due to two factors. First, most people had a personal insurance agent—someone, perhaps even a relative, they knew personally and trusted. The second was that someone personally met with the insured or claimant after a loss. Even on relatively minor claims an adjuster would take detailed statements about what had happened, review the coverage with the insured to show whether the loss was covered or not, and process the claim quickly. Adjusters were not expected to come to the office on the days they were in the field or on the street adjusting claims. Each claim was personal to the claimant or insured.

In the late 1960s a change occurred in the way courts accepted evidence. They began to accept statements about losses that had been recorded over the telephone. This immediately changed the way insurance companies handled claims. No longer was the adjuster automatically dispatched to the home of an insured or claimant; she might never leave the office. Damaged autos and other property were inspected not by the adjuster, but by specially trained appraisers in all but major losses. The former property claim adjusting arms of insurance companies, such as General Adjustment Bureau or Underwriters Adjusting Co., became independent adjusting firms. Instead of visiting injured workers, claimants, or policyholders and consulting with their treating physicians, medical information was obtained by mail or by specialists such as nurses or rehabilitation consultants. Many medical bills were audited by computer. The adjuster had little or no personal contact with the parties who filed claims or were otherwise involved in them. Soon claim adjusters were no longer even called adjusters. They became "the next available claims representative" at the end of some 1-800-HOT LINE, in an office hundreds—or thousands—of miles from the loss location with a computer video display terminal.

By the 1980s the production of insurance likewise had changed. Prior to the 1970s most personal and commercial insurance was placed through local brokers and agents. In the 1970s mergers of brokerage firms resulted in large national organizations that focused primarily on national corporations or governmental agencies and institutions. At the same time, corporate insurance managers became corporate risk managers, and alternative forms of risk financing emerged.

Many agencies remained available to service personal clients and local businesses, but new marketing techniques—ranging from telemarketing to direct mail and Internet sales—drew potential policyholders away from a seemingly more expensive agency system. States also began to permit banks to market insurance, a practice that had been resisted for decades by insurers. These types of changes continued and, in the late 1990s, a number of large brokerage firms that handled primarily commercial accounts merged, again reducing competition for corporate business.

Many insureds began to select price over service, often forfeiting help from an experienced agent or broker. Whether telemarketing, direct marketing, or Internet selling could offer the same degree of selection and advice seemed not to matter.

The net result was that, in the late twentieth century, attitudes toward the insurance industry hardened. Surveys such as those conducted by the Consumers Union showed that the policyholders' approval rate for insurers had dropped considerably, in some cases below 50 percent. One such survey showed that less than 35 percent held a high regard for the industry. Books such as Andrew Tobias's *The Invisible Bankers: Everything the Insurance Industry Never Wanted You to Know* (Linden Press 1982) revealed an insurance industry with massive problems. Some of the problems involved reserving practices, and there were numerous warnings that the industry was ill prepared to weather major losses such as might occur from a series of hurricanes. Both large and small insurance companies were facing financial difficulties, with combined loss ratios running well above 105 percent (spending $105 for every $100 charged in premium). Only relatively high interest rates helped to keep the industry solvent, but many smaller companies still fell by the roadside with their razzle-dazzle of promise becoming little more than another series of claims against state guaranty funds.

Public reaction often took the form of attorney representation for even minor claims. Hiring a lawyer had always been a right, and insurance litigation was nothing new. What was new was that attorneys representing plaintiffs in personal injury cases began advertising their services on television, on billboards, and on bus signs. In the late 1960s the first million-dollar verdict, against a beverage distributor in a Miami claim, was made public. The fact that the plaintiff had been rendered a quadriple-gic seemed not to matter. An insurance claim became like a lottery. "You, too," the ads seemed to suggest, "might have a claim worth a million dollars!"

Public Attitudes

In the late twentieth century, attitudes toward the insurance industry hardened. Surveys such as those conducted by the Consumers Union showed that policyholders' approval rates for insurers had dropped considerably, in some cases below 50 percent.

The Information Age and Insurance Practices

Modern social prophets, such as Alvin Toffler (*Future Shock,* Random House, 1970, and *The Third Wave,* Wm. Morrow & Co., Inc., 1980) told us that electronic communication was the wave of the future. For the most part, what Toffler prophesized thirty years ago is here today. Many Americans log on daily for email and Internet access, converse on wireless cellular telephones, and receive messages on multipurpose pagers. People rarely answer phone calls to businesses. We listen to menus and leave voice mail.

Our televisions offer 100 or more cable or satellite channels, but often not much seems worth watching. While some people rarely read books any more, they may listen to them on tape while sitting in the daily traffic jam. A number of workers use computer workstations at home and telecommute.

What affect has this had on the insurance industry and its ethics? On the negative side, the industry's impersonal nature is growing. Many see the managed care industry as a prime example of a frustratingly impersonal industry. There have been news features about insurance companies that use outside vendors to electronically audit and then challenge medical treatment that should be covered by health policies. Computerized claim negotiation services allow the insurer and a claimant's attorney to negotiate settlements over the Internet without ever meeting with each other. Insurance journals warn agents and brokers to start using e-commerce to market insurance products or risk losing their marketshare.

On the other hand, the electronic lifestyle has many positive features. Home offices mean less traveling, fewer accidents, and lower auto insurance costs. Telecommuting also may result in fewer occupational injuries and lower workers compensation rates.

24-hour Coverage?

Is the idea of combining occupational and nonoccupational medical coverage into a 24-hour coverage package ethical?

This also could hasten the arrival of twenty-four-hour medical coverage combining occupational and nonoccupational illness and injury coverage. Such a combination may be extremely ethical, eliminating the need for businesses and insurers to carry three wallets—one to pay for workers compensation claims, one for employee benefits, and a third for the legal system required to designate which wallet will pay each claim.

This is not likely to occur soon, however. Many interests are involved in the arena of occupational/nonoccupational disputes. In addition, health insurance, especially that offered through employee benefit programs, is the subject of federal regulation under ERISA (The Employee Retirement Income Security Act of 1974). Most occupational injury and disease matters are subject to state Department of Labor workers compensation commissions, which are separate bureaucratic systems from ERISA. Whether such separations and limitations are ethical in the twenty-first century is one issue that remains to be determined.

Simply a Financial Mechanism

As discussed in the next chapter, insurance is simply one method of financing risk, often the method of last resort in a commercial risk management program. There are many methods to finance pure and speculative risks. Most of it is done out of pocket, but some is financed through credit, budgeting, or savings. Insurance should be used only for large, unexpected losses. In some situations, such as premises exposures, smaller types of claims that frequently occur, such as slip-fall accidents, may be insured because of the potential for serious injury. A burned out light bulb is a casualty, but we don't make insurance claims for new light bulbs unless, perhaps, the bulb is an airplane beacon atop a 500-foot tower that costs a few thousand dollars to replace.

When the insurance mechanism is viewed by both the industry and the public as simply a reputable means of financing only extraordinary losses that cannot be financed in more common ways, a large step has been taken toward improving insurance ethics. The problem is that, because most people have to pay insurance premiums of one sort or another, they want to get something back. This leads to unethical behavior on the part of policyholders and third-party claimants who claim minor losses or inconveniences that should be handled in some other way. That, in turn, results in unethical reactions by insurance representatives who begin to view any claim—legitimate or otherwise—in a negative light.

Do you agree?

Even when considered with banks and stockbrokers, insurance is unique. It should hold a position of the highest level of trust, even higher than that to which banks and investment counselors are held.

Insurance is many things, including peace of mind, available capital, and a risk financing source of last resort. It is—perhaps properly so in light of the recent financial combinations—ultimately a financial institution, somewhat like a bank or an investment security firm. Yet, even in company with banks and stockbrokers, insurance is unique. It should hold a position of the highest level of trust, even higher than that to which banks and investment counselors are held.

Thought Provokers

1. Do you believe that an insurance policy that offers benefits to cover losses sustained in business ventures (usually referred to as financial guarantee insurance) meets the criteria of an insurable peril?

2. *Integrity* implies a wholeness, being the same on and off the job. Could a person who is outwardly charming, helpful, and caring at the office but stingy, crabby, and callous with her family be considered an ethical person?

3. Ancient societies managed their risks by joining together for common defense and aid, and by appointing a leader who, either individually or with the counsel of the community, enacted statutes of behavior. In what ways is the institution of insurance an outgrowth of this process?

4. Do you believe that the insurance industry in the twenty-first century is as concerned with finding, reducing, and eliminating causes of loss as it was in earlier centuries?

5. What do you consider to be the primary motivation of those who operate insurance companies in the twenty-first century?

6. Do you believe people are more litigious in the twenty-first century than in prior centuries? If so, why?

7. Do you believe that the trend toward e-commerce in the insurance industry has any effect on the ethics of the insurance industry?

Chapter 2

The Profession of Insurance
in the Twenty-first Century

"The individual practitioners in the established professions are distinguished by the fact that they are in possession of a unique or highly specialized body of knowledge relating directly to their profession and not possessed by those outside the profession."

Dr. Edwin S. Overman
"The Professional Concept and Business Ethics"
American Institute for CPCU

Most insurance operations occur behind the scenes. The general public rarely comes into direct contact with insurance company employees who underwrite, audit, perform actuarial reviews, do computer analysis, administer, or otherwise deal with the insurance product. According to the U.S. Department of Labor about 1 percent of the American labor force worked in the insurance industry as of the late 1990s. Other estimates place the number of people in insurance-related jobs at closer to 10 percent. Considering all those who deal with insurers—such as body shop managers, physicians and their staffs, human resource personnel, and others—the 10 percent figure may be more accurate.

Except for those who are directly or indirectly involved in insurance, most Americans have contact with insurance companies in only two ways. One is when they purchase an insurance product—or review products selected by their employers—and the second is when they have a claim. Therefore, the impression the public has of the industry and its ethics hinges largely on those two situations.

Premium rate increases and adverse media publicity also may influence attitudes, generally in a negative direction. If an individual's experiences have been pleasant, fair, and helpful, his response will be favorable; if, on the other hand, he finds the service to be slow, bureaucratic, outwardly unfair, or arbitrary, he will view the industry as a necessary evil at best. It therefore is advantageous for those who sell and service the insurance product to strive toward ethical professionalism.

Insurance in Modern Society

Insurance has become a necessity of life for most, along with food, shelter, transportation, and occupation. It is not a luxury for the rich. Whether the insurance is on homes and their contents, automobiles, health, or lives, most Americans come into contact with an insurance company to either purchase coverage or make claims.

Yet there are many who, for a variety of reasons, remain uninsured for some or all risks. How do uninsured people survive? Through society, for society is the insurer of last resort, either through governmental programs or private charities. Governmental agencies at all levels, for example, operate health care facilities and hospitals for the physically and mentally ill at taxpayer expense. There are state-operated unemployment compensation and Aid to Families with Dependent Children programs, outgrowths of the Social Security Act, to provide benefits to such families. However, welfare has been reduced in recent years, which may be one of the causes of homelessness. The estimate of the number of homeless people— including families with children—in the United States in the twenty-first century is in the thousands nationwide. Charities may open their doors for such people, but many remain on the street. For these individuals, insurance is unimaginable, unavailable, and definitely unaffordable.

But, as seen in Chapter 1, the insurance industry has become absolutely necessary for a progressive society.

Other Hazards

Decisions not to prevent losses because insurance is available to pay for them become as much an unethical moral and morale hazard as is outward greed or fraud.

For those not forced to take advantage of social programs, purchasing insurance is part of normal life. A typical family may have a score or more insurance policies. Many Americans, after paying for these policies, consider themselves premium poor and question the cost if they rarely make a claim. Others, however, seem too willing to file claims.

Decisions not to prevent losses because insurance is available to pay for them become as much an unethical moral and morale hazard as is outward greed or fraud. We look at the insurance fraud issue in more detail in Chapter 4 because the subject is vital in our attitudes toward insurers. When someone views a claim as an opportunity for gain rather than indemnification, the function of insurance is twisted. Therein lies an ethical dilemma for both the insured and the insurer.

Insurance permits growth and commerce. Without insurance on the collateral for unanticipated losses, lenders would not write mortgages or extend credit. Without insurance on automobiles, there would be chaos on the highways, and few would be able to afford new vehicles. Our entire transportation-based economy would falter. Without health insurance millions would fall into poverty. Without life insurance few families could weather the loss of a parent.

Large insurance groups, in company with their companion banking and investment firms, have become the financial backbone of the nation. Without them few businesses could afford to venture into new enterprises. Without insurance, neither families nor commercial and governmental entities could prosper. Of course, government could do all that insurance now does, but only by taxing at a much higher level. Many would consider that to be an unethical option.

For these reasons insurance has to be more than just commerce, more than just another business. Its ethical role in the community must be considered.

The Role of Insurance in Enterprise Risk Management

Much has been written in the last few years about new commercial risk management techniques. Dr. George L. Head, director emeritus of the Insurance Institute of America in Malvern, Pennsylvania, writing in the *National Underwriter, P&C Edition* (June 5, 2000), refers to *enterprise risk management.* This is one of the relatively new buzzwords within the risk industry, the objective of which is predictable cash flow. He says, "[M]ost of the truly disruptive unanticipated events an organization experiences arise from technological, market or competitive changes, not accidental loss." He adds that in the twenty-first century the risk concern will be "net cash flow" rather than "cost of risk."

Other newer phrases include *alternative risk financing* techniques and *integrated* risk management, which are intended to reflect changes in the way commercial entities handle their risks. In today's global, electronic business world, new techniques, new resources, and new methods of dealing with risk are necessary. Commerce is no longer local. It is international, and the methods of managing the risks of such commerce also are international. This can pose ethical questions.

Until the late 1960s commercial entities had insurance managers to manage the insurance policies. As the insurance industry went through cycles of price cutting and less diligent underwriting, and then financial difficulties and price increases with stricter underwriting, many commercial entities began to select alternative means of managing risks. While loss control had always been a safety consideration, it now became a financing factor. The concept of managing risk by a combination of loss control and risk financing factors, each carefully blended to achieve the best financial result, arose. Insurance played a less important role, and those in charge of the program were called *risk* managers.

Global Implications

Commerce is no longer local. It is international, and the methods of managing the risks of such commerce also are international. This can pose ethical questions.

By the end of the twentieth century the process again had evolved, and risk management was viewed even more as a financial function. The title of Chief Risk Officer (CRO) arose as the individual responsible for *speculative risks* as well as traditional risks associated with insurance. Losses or gains in investments, foreign currency fluctuations, over-demand due to under-production, and similar concerns were beginning to fall within the realm of risk management.

One result of such changes may be that a greater burden is placed on insurance representatives to assist a finance-oriented CRO identify exposures, select appropriate risk finance and control methods, and carefully monitor traditional losses. Unless the CRO has a well-trained loss control staff, traditional and alternative risk financing experts, and claims personnel, she is likely to rely to a greater extent on the insurer's representatives. That opens the door to opportunities for unethical behavior in taking advantage of a CRO's needs.

Insurance is simply a method of financing loss by contractual transfer. There are a number of ways to transfer the risk of loss by contract. Individuals, businesses, and governments daily enter into contracts. Many contain transfer mechanisms such as hold harmless agreements, indemnification clauses, and waivers of subrogation that transfer liability for loss from one party to another. There are a number of ethical issues involved in such transfers.

For transfers of risk to be ethical, the parties involved need to be in complete agreement as to what risk is being transferred and its financial implications. People who enter leases or rental agreements may not read the fine print of the contract and later find that they have accepted a risk unknowingly. The courts will not excuse such ignorance. Unless the contract was entered fraudulently, it usually will be upheld.

Such contracts frequently involve insurance requirements as a means to finance the transfer of risk, and insurance representatives of the parties often become involved in resolving contractual disputes. All of the involved parties, from the insureds and claimants to the brokers, agents, underwriters, and claim adjusters, must fully review and understand contractual agreements and comply with them to the extent that coverage exists on the insurance policy. For example, if an adjuster ignores an *additional insured* endorsement on a liability policy, the insurer may be found to be in bad faith by a court. (See "Additional Insureds—The Case of the Deadly Endorsement," *CPCU Claims Quarterly*, Vol. 15, No. 3, Aug. 1997, for court citations.)

Insurance: Primary Protection or Last Resort?

When either an individual or a commercial risk considers the insurance program to be the first risk financing resource, it is likely that ethical issues will evolve. The role of insurance is to protect against the losses that cannot reasonably be weathered alone. These include the disasters and calamities that can arise out of automobile wrecks; house or office fires; hurricanes and earthquakes; defective and dangerous products; major pollution spills; and diseases requiring expensive treatment or surgery, a long disability, or the death of or permanent injury to a breadwinner. It is the catastrophe, the unusual, the purely accidental occurrences that are ethically the subject of insurance, not the burned-out light bulb type of loss.

This, in part, may explain why certain aspects of managed care have been less than well received by the public and subject to both media and governmental criticism. The concept of managed care is to a certain extent a *loss control* process, built partly on the concept of preventive medicine. By utilizing the same health maintenance organization (HMO) for all care—both routine preventive procedures and serious diseases and injuries—at a single fixed price, the insurance mechanism designed for the serious and expensive situation is diluted by the cost of routine and nonserious care.

Therefore, when a serious illness or injury does occur, the HMO is forced to employ cost-cutting procedures and make judgments that ultimately may harm the patient. This makes the HMO accept more patients who are not seriously ill to cover the costs associated with a seriously ill patient, which leads to HMO physicians spending less time with individual patients. This opens an HMO and its insurer administrators to disputes over the ethics of the care that is provided.

Do You Agree?

The concept of managed care is to a certain extent a loss control process, built partly on the concept of preventive medicine.

Abuse by insureds who over-utilized the health care system as much as medical cost inflation may have led to the insurance industry's adoption of managed medical care programs. It can be argued that primary medical care is not an insurable peril at all, for it lacks criteria such as fortuity and seriousness. If an insurability criterion is that the loss must be serious enough to impose financial hardship, then certainly the costs associated with much disease and injury—including hospitalization, surgery, and medications—do qualify. But routine medical visits, even for a specific disease, may not. Could this be a reason that managed care operations have been accused of making unethical choices and denying coverage to seriously ill patients while paying for routine physicals for healthy insureds?

The Opposite

Just as insurance should not be a first resort for every minor loss, neither should it be the ultimate means of absorbing the most disastrous of losses. Some losses may be so disastrous as to be incalculable, again one of the criteria for insurability. Insurance is a risk-financing tool; risk control is needed as well if an ethical result is to occur. Few insurance programs can cover totally devastating loss.

Insurance deals with many types of risks where an uncontrolled disaster could tax all of a commercial insured's available primary and excess insurance as well as the reinsurance backing them. One is the *highly protected risk*, usually a business with high property values in which the insured has invested substantial loss control. Such coverages usually come with fairly high deductibles.

The risk of a *total* loss might be so expensive, but also so remote, that the owners do not or could not economically insure to full value. To deal with such situations, insurers often impose conditions such as a *coinsurance clause*. When a complete and total loss is extremely remote, the insurer might agree to pay losses above a deductible up to the policy limits if the insured carries coverage that meets a certain percentage of the total property value. If the insured carries less than that percentage, he shares in the loss to the extent of that ratio. Coinsurance is a logical and ethical means of providing protection without undue exposure to the insurer or excessive cost to the insured.

For liability risks, a somewhat different approach to ultimate possible exposure must be considered. Liability risks can devastate an entire industry, and when such devastation has not been taken into consideration by both the insureds and their insurers, chaos can result. An example of this is the asbestos industry, which for years saw itself as a positive factor in the safeguarding of America. Asbestos was fireproof, and it was used in schools and other public buildings as a loss control product. After the 1908 Collingwood School fire in Cleveland, in which 174 students and teachers died, use of asbestos was considered a remarkable improvement in loss prevention. However, in the 1970s it was discovered that thousands of Americans who had worked with or around asbestos had acquired a fatal lung disease, asbestosis, and use of the mineral was banned. Companies that had manufactured asbestos products were sued, and most turned to their insurance companies to defend them and finance the settlements and judgments.

This led to one of the most serious insurance crises of the twentieth century, the question of what constituted an *accident* or *occurrence* under a liability policy. Similar issues also arose over other pollution-related claims, and the nation's courts were jammed with litigation. Many manufacturers who became embroiled in pollution litigation—regardless of whether or not they were found to be insured for resulting claims—found that the insurance they carried was insufficient protection. Many declared bankruptcy and were reorganized by the courts in order to remain in business.

Last Resort?

Insurance may be the last resort of financing loss, but it cannot be expected to cover all costs of every calamity. It is the ethical obligation of the agent, broker, or claims representative to explain limitations as much as possible before loss occurs.

Could such issues have been handled more ethically? Were insureds and their insurance companies correct in pursuing every issue in the courts? The cases spawned many questions that focus directly on the issue of insurance ethics. One such issue is that of *reasonable expectation.* What might an insured reasonably anticipate from the language of an insurance policy? Did the insurers meet that expectation? Did each of the parties act in *good faith?*

Insurance may be the last resort of financing loss, but it cannot be expected to cover all costs of every calamity. There have to be limitations and exclusions, and it is necessary for every insured to understand what those are. It is the ethical obligation of the agent, broker, or claims representative to explain those limitations, as much as possible before loss occurs.

The Practice of Insurance: Marketing and Claims

Ethical issues arise at every point in the marketing and claim process. Thousands of businesses found that the insurance representatives they had carefully selected no longer were in business after the mergers and acquisitions among brokerage firms in the mid-1990s. Their accounts had been transferred to another entity. When insured businesses merged or were acquired, similar insurance muddles arose. Which brokerage firm would be retained? Which policies should be kept and which cancelled? How would new claims that arose from situations that occurred prior to the acquisition be covered? Each of these issues raised ethical questions.

Many claims have a long tail. The loss may occur in one policy period, but the claim may not be settled until many years later. When agents or brokers merge, or when a commercial insured selects a new agent or broker to take over its account, records can become lost; the prior broker may have little, if any, interest in helping a former client resolve coverage matters. That agent or broker, nevertheless, has an ethical—and perhaps a legal—obligation to continue to service prior client's needs.

An equally serious ethical situation can arise from another aspect of marketing: the failure to assess the customer's needs and properly address them. The insurance agent or broker—or the insurer itself in a direct marketing program—has a duty to understand the customer's needs and offer products that will fill those needs. To either fail to explain why a coverage is needed or why it is being offered is as unethical as attempting to sell a product that is not needed, is redundant, or is more costly than necessary.

> **Is this Unethical?**
>
> *To either fail to explain why a coverage is needed or why it is being offered is as unethical as attempting to sell a product that is not needed, is redundant, or is more costly than necessary.*

The other side of the insurance equation is that of claim service. It is the insurer's claim representative who embodies the policy contract, regardless of whether that representative is an outside defense attorney hired to represent the insured in a lawsuit, an attorney employed directly by the insurer, a company adjuster, an independent adjuster assigned a claim for outside investigation, or simply a voice at the end of a telephone line. The claim representative has a duty to investigate, evaluate, and negotiate first the coverage, then the liability, and finally the damages. It is often within these steps that ethical issues arise. Typical breaches include denial of coverage when it should apply, failure to investigate a contractual or statutory offset for a claim, and being too arbitrary regarding depreciation on a property loss. There are thousands of ways that a claim can be mishandled, and many involve decisions that are not ethical. Many of these are explored in later chapters.

Aspects of a Profession

Professionals often are easy to spot. It is easy to envision the registered nurse in a crisp white uniform, a physician in a long white coat, or a surgeon in a green scrub suit. While attorneys no longer wear wigs and white tab collars in America, judges still wear black robes. We might assume that a person at a construction site wearing a shirt, tie, and hard hat and carrying a clipboard is an engineer or architect. We recognize clergy by their clerical collars, and airline pilots or ship captains by their uniforms.

There is no specific uniform for insurance agents or claim adjusters. They look just like any other businessperson. There are no trappings of a profession—the required membership in a professional society, the board certification, a universal requirement for many hours of continuing education, the stack of professional journals that must be read, the *pro bono* cases carried. And often there are no rewards of a profession either. Few adjusters drive luxury cars, live in mansions, own ocean-going yachts, or vacation for a few months on the French Riviera.

Is insurance a profession or just a business? Dr. Edwin S. Overman, former president of the American Institute for Chartered Property Casualty Underwriters, posed one of the most definitive answers to this question in his essay, "The Professional Concept and Business Ethics." Overman outlined several criteria that separate a true profession from other vocations. These include:

1. The importance of a highly unified body of specialized knowledge;

2. The significance of a broad educational background containing generalized knowledge;

3. The necessity of a carefully conceived Code of Personal Ethics;

4. A need to strive for the ideal of altruistic attitude and behavior;

5. The role of searching examinations to discern mastery in the specialized skills of the profession; and

6. The role of the professional organization to control entry to that profession and to monitor the professional's continuing adherence to the tenets of that profession.

Add another condition to Overman's list: the need for careful mentoring of the professional by her colleagues as she ventures into the selected field. This may be implicit in the role of the professional society.

A vocation in the insurance industry falls far short of meeting Overman's criteria. At best an insurance career is a professional vocation, for there are many professionals within it. Even though most states license certain insurance practitioners, and those who are attorneys may be members of the Bar, insurance itself is not a profession. A graduate degree is not required for agents or adjusters, although graduate study in insurance and risk management is available at many universities. A background of generalized knowledge is not even required, and there are many within the insurance industry who have little or no college experience. Those with college degrees have often specialized in business administration, still falling short of the "broad educational background containing generalized knowledge" criterion suggested by Overman. Lack of a background in the liberal arts may hamper the communication skills necessary in dealing with different types of individuals, especially those who have suffered a loss of some sort.

> **Do You Agree?**
>
> *Insurance itself is not a profession. At best an insurance career is a professional vocation, for there are many professionals within it.*

There are many insurance organizations, including some with educational requirements, but none of them control membership in the industry. Many states do require licensing and continuing education, but the licensing is often as much a form of revenue raising as it is a careful review of the licensee. The stringency of continuing education varies from one region to another. To suggest that insurance is a true profession is somewhat ludicrous.

All this is not to say that insurance ought not to be a profession. The importance of the insurance industry to society clearly and ethically mandates that it should be a profession, and every member within it should be a true professional. However, until that day arrives, insurance will simply be a career, a vocation, a job.

> A desk job! Is that all you can see in it? Just a hard chair to park your pants on from nine to five? Just a pile of papers to shuffle around and sharp pencils and a scratch pad to make figures on, with maybe a little doodling on the side? That's not the way I see it, Walter. To me, a claims man is a surgeon, and that desk is an operating table, and those pencils are scalpels and bone chisels. And those papers are not just forms and statistics and claims for compensation. They're alive! They're packed with drama,

with twisted hopes and crooked dreams. A claims man, Walter, is a doctor and a bloodhound and a cop and a judge and a jury and a father confessor all in one.

Edward G. Robinson speaking toFred MacMurray in
Double Indemnity
Directed by Billy Wider for Paramount, 1944

Perhaps today too many young insurance people do see the field as simply a desk job, stuck behind a computer in a small cubicle, required to produce whatever the assigned task may be. Could this be a question of ethics on a larger scale, that of the industry as a whole? Why should those in the insurance industry who deal with the public be held to professional ethical standards if insurance is not a profession?

Even in the original version of the *Oath of Hippocrates* the rule is restrictive: "To impart to my children and the children of the master who taught me and the disciples who have been enrolled and agreed to the rules of the profession, *but to these alone,* the precepts and the instructions." Perhaps insurance should be open *only* to those who have studied at postgraduate level, mastered the skills of insurance, and passed examinations to enter into a professional society that controls the right to work in the industry. Until that day we cannot truthfully refer to insurance as a true profession.

Insurance Education and Licensing

Many who argue that insurance is a profession often point to the many state licensing and bonding requirements, the need for professional liability insurance, and the availability of local insurance-related associations. However, dogs and automobiles also are licensed and there are exams for plumbers and electricians and auto emission control inspectors. Travel agents purchase professional liability insurance, but they consider themselves to be in a business, not a profession.

The insurance industry does invest a considerable amount of money to prepare people for their jobs and to inform them of changes. Most of this is termed training. It is not *education*, nor does it generally impart the "highly unified body of specialized knowledge" required for a profession. That is rarely its intent. Training is intended to teach the student *how* to do the task assigned. Education is intended to teach a student *why*. When he learns why something is important, learning how to do it is easy.

Real insurance education is time-consuming and costly. It requires professional commitment both by instructors and students. Yet it is available, both through many of the nation's universities and through insurance institutions such as The American College, which administers the Chartered Life Underwriter designation program; the American Institute for CPCU and the Insurance Institute of America, which grants the Chartered Property Casualty Underwriter designation and a number of associate designations; and the College of Insurance, which issues graduate and postgraduate degrees in risk management and insurance. The Society of Insurance Trainers and Educators (SITE) identifies sixty-nine separate insurance professional designations, most of which require class attendance, study, and the passing of written examinations.

> **How or Why?**
>
> *Training is intended to teach the student how to do the task assigned. Education is intended to teach a student why. When a person learns why something is important, learning how to do it is easy.*

Given all this, it is difficult to argue that insurance is not a profession. However, while many within the field are professionals and have earned such designations, neither the insurance industry nor the public, through its state regulatory arm, demands that practitioners have even one of these designations—nor even an undergraduate degree. They are all voluntary.

Public Law 15 and its Effect on the Insurance Industry

Every state maintains an insurance department. These regulatory agencies have authority over insurance company admittance and operation in their respective states. Most states license insurance agents and brokers, and many also license both company and independent claim adjusters. The director or commissioner of the state agency is almost always a member of the National Association of Insurance Commissioners (NAIC), which provides a forum for developing uniform legislation.

Even though insurance is a national and international enterprise, it is regulated by the states. The reason for this is found in a history that makes insurance ethics significant today.

While most businesses are not regulated, insurance has been seen as more than just another business—it plays a significant role in the nation's well being. States do charter businesses, however, and insurance companies likewise had to be registered in the states where they did business. Several New England states established separate insurance commissions in the 1850s. In 1866 a bill was introduced in Congress to establish a federal insurance regulatory agency within the Treasury Department, but the bill never passed.

In the 1860s a man named Samuel Paul became an agent for a number of New York insurance companies. Virginia law required agents for nonresident insurers to be licensed and to deposit securities with the state. Paul refused. He transacted business without the license, was arrested, and fined $50. The case was appealed and eventually wound up in the Supreme Court.

In *Paul v. Virginia,* 75 U.S. 168 (1869), the Court made two significant findings. First, it found that corporations are not citizens within the meaning of the equal rights clause and that insurance was *not commerce* within the meaning of the interstate commerce clause of the U.S. Constitution. Therefore, insurance was not subject to federal antitrust laws. This ruling held for more than seventy years, when it was overruled.

In 1942 the State of Missouri alleged a rate-making conspiracy and got the Antitrust Division of the U.S. Department of Justice to challenge the South-Eastern Underwriters Association, a rate-setting organization, under the Sherman Antitrust Act. Ultimately the U.S. Supreme Court reversed the longstanding rule and found that insurance was commerce and subject to all federal laws and regulations (*United States v. South-Eastern Underwriters Association,* 322 U.S. 533 [1944]). Federal antitrust regulations would dictate that any sharing of loss data, mortality tables, or other shared data to establish reasonable rates would be illegal. Congress was besieged with industry lobbyists; doom and gloom, along with chaos, was predicted.

The result was *Public Law 15,* (March 9, 1945) the McCarran-Ferguson Act, which established that state regulation and taxation of the insurance industry was in the public interest. It states that as long as the states actively regulate insurance, the federal government cannot do so.

This legislation has been challenged many times in the last half-century but remains in force today. Nevertheless, it creates many kinds of conflicts within the industry, especially since insurance companies have been merged into banking and security investment firms that are subject to federal regulation. In addition, many employee benefit insurance programs are subject to the federal Employee Retirement Income Security Act of 1974 (ERISA). Federal courts have limited the rights of states to involve themselves in disputes involving insurance programs subject to ERISA.

Insurance and the Law: Legislation and Regulation

All states have an insurance code that regulates how insurance companies do business in the state. One important function of these departments is to approve insurance rates. The structure and ethics of insurance rates is discussed in Chapter 3.

The codes create the departments of insurance and assign to the primary insurance regulator the task of being the state's chief insurance fire marshal. In some states the regulator, called a director or commissioner, is elected; in other states she is appointed. As a result, the position is almost always highly political.

The state regulator also has a legislative role: to propose insurance laws or code amendments. He is not only subject to lobbying by insurance organizations but also must lobby state legislatures for new laws. Questions about the ethics of lobbying are as prevalent for insurance regulation and legislation as for Congress.

Litigation

As discussed in Chapter 1, an insured who believes she has been treated unfairly by an insurance company has a common law right to sue the insurer. Additionally, the United States common law system permits any party to sue any other party for any alleged offense. The United States system of tort law, which is discussed in Chapter 6, permits litigation over nearly any alleged negligent act that causes any alleged damage.

Insurance Research Council (Malvern, Pennsylvania) data from the late 1990s shows that unrepresented claimants receive a higher net recovery on average than represented claimants and that they receive settlements months earlier. Nevertheless third-party attorney representation remains high in the twenty-first century. Movements toward tort reform, such as limitations on punitive damage awards and venue shopping, have been promoted by the casualty insurance industry. Yet it is largely that industry's own clients that resist change. Insurers often view plaintiff attorneys—referred to as the trial bar—as their enemy, but those attorneys often represent the insurers' own customers. Can it be ethical to view a customer as a potential enemy? Is American litigiousness—an eagerness to sue—out of control?

Plaintiff Attorneys

Insurers often view plaintiff attorneys as their enemy, but those attorneys often represent the insurers' own customers. Can it be ethical to view a customer as a potential enemy? Is American litigiousness—an eagerness to sue—out of control?

One thing that has not changed in America's 225-plus-year history is a devotion to the principle that Americans have a right to sue for that which they believe they are entitled. The following excerpt describing the atmosphere in the early 1800s shows this:

Stafford v. Lucas, a suit for damages, dismissed by the court. *Davenport v. Archer,* damages, dismissed. *Holt v. Mason,* slander, settled. *Orr v. Miller,* removal for cause. *Miller v. Riggs,* theft of valuable property, jury found for defendant. *Gregg v. Miller,* breach of contract of debt, verdict for plaintiff. *Butler v. Thompson,* debt for goods and merchandise, plus labor, plaintiff verdict with award. *Orr v. Wead,* damages to Orr because Wead had agreed to teach Orr the "art and mystery" of weaving and had breached the contract. Defendant produced documentation of previous settlement of suit; case dismissed with award of costs to Wead.

It's the stuff of daily courtroom battle. We've grown litigious and quarrelsome, eager to take our neighbor to court over every minor issue and sue for damages. The courts are burdened; time and again the citizens are called for jury duty and most take valuable time from work to hear all this nonsense. Is it not time for reform and change in our legal system? We're suing ourselves to death.

Who? Us? No, Stafford, and Davenport, Holt and Orr. Miller, and Gregg, and Butler. Ohio was not yet a year old when the Common Pleas Court of Montgomery County heard these actions in 1803 and 1804. Aaron Burr had yet to duel with Alexander Hamilton. Ohio, carved out of the woods, was sparsely populated, and the scattering of the native tribes by General "Mad Anthony" Wayne had been only ten years earlier.

The German settlers who faithfully served as jurors at these trials had only recently arrived from "Dutch" or Dunkard villages in Pennsylvania, Virginia, or the Upper Rhine Valley. Nearly 200 years ago they stood in the midst of Dayton's wilderness, suing the ass off each other— literally. Brumbaugh brought suit because he'd loaned George a mare for a trip from Dayton to St. Mary's; he alleged that George "immoderately drove, beat and abused" the horse so badly that it died. He wanted George's jackass as compensation, and the jury awarded it to him.

How many people could there have been when the same people were called for jury duty in virtually every court session? Maybe a thousand in the whole county? The records from later than 1810 show only 600 families. In 1803 they met in Newcom's Tavern, a four-room log cabin. One room was the court. A second was where the judge and all the lawyers slept. Prisoners in criminal cases were kept in the corn crib. Damages were awarded in nearly half the cases. Lawyers in attendance included a future governor of Ohio. It was a raucous good time for all!

> "Are Our Courts Really Out of Control?"
> *Claims Magazine,* August, 1995

The American legal system is very much a religion: it has all the elements of ritual, drama, good and bad, light and dark, and even human sacrifice—at least in a capital case. The objective is *Truth,* but truth is often the victim.

Thought Provokers

1. Is a career in insurance a *profession* in the same category as law, medicine, or the clergy? Should it be?

2. The insurance industry has become an integral part of the nation's financial network, much of which is federally regulated. Should the federal government regulate insurance, or should the states retain insurance regulation?

3. Lobbying is a political practice in which proponents of an issue attempt to persuade those in control that their position is correct. Lobbying often includes activities such as campaign contributions and contact with involved politicians in social settings. Is it ethical for the insurance industry to be involved in lobbying?

4. Should all insurance agents, brokers, and adjusters have a particular graduate degree and be members of a national insurance professional society before being licensed?

5. The concept of managed medical care has been adopted in the insurance industry for other areas, such as legal services and auto or home damage repairs. Are such trends positive or negative?

Chapter 3
Is the Customer Always Right?

*"The customer is often wrong, because he or she
rarely understands what is needed. A better slogan
would be, 'The customer's best interests must always
come first'."*

The Claims-conscious Iconoclast

The two situations in which the public comes into direct contact with the insurance industry are

1. when coverage is purchased, and

2. when a loss occurs and a claim is made.

While the need for ethical behavior permeates the entire industry, it is in these two arenas that the industry's standards enter the spotlight.

Many otherwise rational individuals often think with their wallet rather than using common sense. There is a principle in marketing—whether right or wrong—that price sells. Practicality suggests, however, that people get only what they pay for. If they pay for quality and the merchant is ethical, they should get a quality product. If, on the other hand, they want only what is cheap, chances are the product may fail when it is most needed. The ancient rule of the marketplace, *caveat emptor*—let the buyer beware!—prevails.

Such a rule, however, cannot ethically be applied to the sale of insurance products for they are intangible and cannot be inspected or experienced prior to use—unless the customer previously had a claim with the same insurer under the same coverage. The insurance customer is purchasing an aleatory contract, an unknown, a promise. In exchange for nothing more than a wad of paper containing that promise, the purchaser is paying a sizable amount. Insurance is not cheap.

It therefore falls to those who market and underwrite insurance to attempt to provide what the customer needs at a price that is both fair and adequate. As discussed in the previous chapter, that requires both imagination and initiative. The customer may not know what she needs; she may be concerned only with price. That puts the seller into an ethical dilemma. Should an agent sell the customer what she says she wants, or should he earnestly attempt to sell what she really needs?

> **Customer Needs Come First**
>
> *It falls to those who market and underwrite insurance to attempt to provide what the customer needs at a price that is both fair and adequate.*

The Basics of Underwriting: Spreading the Risk

The criteria for insurable perils were outlined in Chapter 1, where it also was noted that the entire insurance system is based on spreading risk among a large number of similar units. This raises many issues, for it is not always clear how *homogeneous* any particular group of similar units might be. We are, for example, all human beings who are genetically similar. Yet some of us are old, some young; we are of different races, colors, gender, appearance, and cultures; our physical conditions, disabilities, diseases, and diets differ. Therefore, needs and exposures in terms of risk of loss also differ.

However, physical items can be similar. All types of automobiles are similar. They operate on gasoline, have four wheels, and operate with a motor. But some are old and others brand new. Some are small sedans and others large trucks or utility vans. Some are very expensive and others less expensive. Some are more hazardous than others. The same is true of homes, places of work, and possessions.

The key to insurance underwriting is the detection and evaluation of these differences within groups of similar units. The information regarding the exposure—a person, an automobile, a dwelling—must be accurate if the underwriter is to make a correct decision on insurability. Serious factors that may affect the ethics of a situation must be considered in every underwriting decision.

For example, most state insurance regulatory agencies have outlawed an underwriting practice called redlining. In this procedure underwriters marked certain areas on a map (presumably in red) to indicate where they would not write insurance coverage, regardless of the true nature of a specific risk. The areas were determined through factors such as the neighborhood racial makeup, age of buildings, crime statistics, or the ability of residents to obtain credit. Occasionally exclusions were made by using postal zip codes. The criteria may have been sound and practical, but the overall result was discriminatory to that neighborhood.

Practices once considered to be sound underwriting continue to make headlines when they involve allegations of discrimination. The *Atlanta (Georgia) Journal-Constitution* reported on Dec. 16, 2000, that a major life insurer in the state was under "a full-blown investigation" because of charges that the insurer had charged black policyholders higher premiums than white policyholders. According to the company, the higher premiums for policies sold between 1930 and 1950 "were based on life expectancy, not race". The company added that, "It is well established in historical actuarial data that there was a direct correlation between race and mortality rates—nonwhite mortality rates were higher than white mortality rates." The insurer also pointed out that during the pre-Civil Rights era various state insurance departments had accepted their mortality tables, including the State of Georgia, which was conducting the investigation.

How Are Decisions Made?

Information is the key. Underwriting decisions must be based on data that is verifiable and actuarially sound.

If such items alone cannot be used as an exclusive consideration, what can be used? Certainly no insurer wants to sell policies when there is a high expectation of loss. Insurers exist for the benefit of their insureds and, in the case of stock companies, for their shareholders. They are not charitable institutions.

Underwriting decisions must be based on verifiable data and actuarially sound criteria. They must be based on *information*. The more information the underwriter has, the more likely he will assign the risk to the proper collection of homogeneous units. When the number of exposures is large enough, factors such as age, sex, and type of building construction or year, or make and model of car, age of drivers, and intent of usage can be grouped and matched against loss experience for that category.

What is the source of information about an individual risk? That is partly what the agent or broker must determine. She must obtain accurate information about the proposed risk from the applicant. That may be as simple as filling out an application form or as complex as submitting a proposal for coverage on a major commercial entity, complete with prior loss data, asset printouts, annual reports, and company brochures. The issues that determine whether the process is ethical are honesty, accuracy, and completeness of information. Even if it is only a form application, answers must be detailed, timely, correct, and without gaps.

Pricing Insurance:
Fair, Adequate, and Nondiscriminatory

An insurance rate consists of a number of factors. The basis of a rate, called the *pure premium*, is the average of all losses incurred within a stated period for a particular classification of risk. A*llocated* expenses, such as the cost of defense in liability policies, must be added to the pure premium. Once this base rate has been established, percentages are added for the insurer's administration, taxes, licenses and other fees, investment and surplus, profit, and agent or broker commission.

According to the Insurance Information Institute's (I.I.I.) *Fact Book 2000,* for every $100 of automobile premium paid in 1998, $9 was used for medical expenses, $1 for wage loss and other economic payments, $6 for pain and suffering, $41 for vehicle damage, $12 for legal fees, and $6 for other costs of settling claims. The cost of company operations took another $5; $2 was spent on taxes, licenses, and other fees; $2 on policyholder dividends; and $17 for commissions and other selling expenses.

The total of all this is $101, or $1 more than the $100 taken in as premium. This is called the *combined ratio.* But the industry did not go broke paying out $101 for every $100 it took in. According to the I.I.I., insurers made $11 on pretax income and netted $7 in profit. If only the costs directly related to indemnifying insureds and claimants were considered, $59 out of the $100 was paid in claims. That is the pure premium on which a rate would be calculated.

Most state insurance codes, which follow NAIC model legislation, mandate that an insurer's rates be actuarially sound, fair, adequate, and nondiscriminatory. Actuarial soundness is achieved by basing rates on accurate (*actual*) loss data correctly calculated.

The other qualifications of fairness, adequacy, and nondiscrimination are a bit more subjective. What is *adequate,* what is *fair,* and what *discriminates* can be in the eye of the beholder?

Professor C. Arthur Williams, Jr., of the University of Minnesota suggested several definitions of unfair as used in a rating statute in his essay, "Unfair Rate Discrimination in Property and Liability Insurance" (Irwin 1969):

> The qualifying adjective "unfair" is generally omitted because, as will become apparent later, price discrimination is a neutral term in economics and to label this practice "unfair" prejudges the practice. On the other hand, because price discrimination does not include all types of price differentiation, the absence of some qualifying adjective is also misleading. Instead of attempting to solve this terminological issue [this essay] will refer to unfair price discrimination because this is the accepted terminology of insurance. [Other definitions do not] indicate (1) where the costs are marginal costs or average costs, or (2) what relationship should exist between prices and costs.

> An insurance rate structure will be considered to be unfairly discriminatory if, allowing for practical limitation, there are premium differences that do not correspond to expected losses and average expenses or if there are expected average cost differences that are not reflected in premium differences.

The state regulator has considerable control over the rates insurance companies may charge for certain types of coverage, such as auto liability and workers compensation insurance. Many times insurers request rate increases to meet rising costs that have been denied by the regulator for what appear to be political reasons. A regulator may be more likely to be elected or reelected by promising to keep rates low.

Insurers ceased writing insurance in several states due to this practice. When insurers refuse to renew auto liability or workers compensation coverages, the policyholders often must turn to more expensive nonadmitted or substandard insurers or enter the assigned risk pool. Therefore, a regulator's refusal to approve a rate can backfire if it causes insurers to cease writing coverage.

Assessing the Customer's Needs

Insurance representatives who market coverage need to accurately assess each customer's needs. This includes all forms of insurance marketing, including Internet and telephone sales. For example, those who create Web sites to sell insurance must include enough selectors so that an unsophisticated consumer must seriously consider all options. Too many such Web sites and brochures are little more than advertising and sales puff, pushing price or convenience rather than the protection offered by the insurance product. Telemarketers, likewise, must be able to ask appropriate questions and to address questions posted to them in order to complete an ethical transaction.

> **Do You Agree?**
>
> *The agent or broker's real product is risk analysis and service, not just the sale of insurance products. Agents should determine the client's needs first. Failure to do this can result in selling the wrong product and a professional liability claim against the agent or broker.*

The agent or broker who meets personally with clients likewise must assess their need for insurance, alternative risk financing, and loss control. The agent or broker's real product is risk analysis and service, not just the sale of insurance products. If the agent or broker is unfamiliar with the insured and the involved risks, he should determine what those needs are. Failure to do this can result in selling the wrong product and a professional liability claim against the agent or broker. (See Chapter 8.)

Danger: Selling the Customer What He Doesn't Need

An insurer's ethical objective must not be to simply sell *more* of what it markets, but to sell the right product to the right customer for the right price. In marketing the product, insurance representatives must consider each insured individually.

There should be some sense of self-preservation in the notion of selling only what a customer needs, for it does not take long for a person to figure out that she has been treated unfairly. A customer lost, marketing authorities suggest, is actually several customers lost, for each angry customer will tell others his story.

But there also are other ethical considerations. For example, a customer who purchases more coverage than he needs may have an ulterior motive. Over-insuring is one of the standard fraud indicators, along with the desire for a quick settlement. To illustrate, someone with a residence that could be rebuilt for $125,000 insures it for $250,000 in a state with a *valued policy law*. If a fire destroys that residence the insurer must pay the full $250,000 regardless of the cost to rebuild. It is very likely that the agent who sold the policy will undergo as stern an investigation as the insured! Selling too much coverage is as unethical as selling the wrong—or insufficient—coverage. Either can get the seller into trouble.

Another example of these principles can be found in a recent investigation into the life insurance business in Georgia and several other states. The investigation uncovered evidence that many people were sold multiple life insurance policies, but, when the insured died, no payments were made on some of the multiple policies because the insurers failed to check their records. These burial policies often were referred to as industrial life insurance policies. Sold on debit routes where the salesman would personally collect the monthly premiums, they were popular in many black and poorer neighborhoods between 1940 and 1960. Face amounts on the policies were generally between $500 and $2000, and the salesmen would encourage insureds to purchase more than one policy to increase the benefits.

Dollar Swapping

One factor that makes a peril insurable is that the loss it produces must be so large that a person or entity could not reasonably bear it alone. When insurance is used either by an individual or commercial entity to cover relatively minor losses and expenses that would not cause economic hardship, the insurance product must be priced extremely high in order to cover the costs of paying and administering such small claims. This, then, becomes little more than a process of dollar swapping, in which the insurer charges a high premium and hopes to make a profit on investments before the money must be repaid to the insured on claims. In general, the higher the deductible, the lower the premium.

Dollar swapping may not even be ethical, for its pricing necessitates a premium far higher than an actuarially sound evaluation of real risk would indicate. It falls short of spreading the risk of fortuitous and serious loss, even if a portion of the premium charged might have that purpose.

Who's in Charge?

Questions about who really is in charge often arise in high deductible insurance programs. Is the insured or the insurer in charge? Such questions arise in both defense and settlement situations. Even when the entire primary layer of protection is self-insured, coverage issues with excess insurers or consideration of entities that are indemnified by contract often lead to litigation.

Many commercial insureds partially self-fund their liability risks using insurance coverage with very high deductibles. This is different from self-insurance. Every claim, regardless of size or whether it falls entirely within the deductible, is subject to the terms of the insurance policy. The insured may believe it can dictate defense and settlement postures because its money, and not the insurance company's, is at stake. But such is not the case. Standard liability and workers compensation policies reserve the right and duty to settle or defend for the insurance company, not the insured.

Therefore, the insured cannot require that the insurer defend a case the insurer believes it should settle—unless there is a consent to settle clause in the policy. In *Lieberman v. Employers Ins. Co. of Wausau,* 419 A.2d 417 (N.J. 1980), for example, the insured's policy contained a consent to settle clause. Lieberman originally approved a settlement but later revoked it in light of new evidence. The court upheld his right to revoke the consent and also held a defense attorney retained by the insurer personally liable for having settled the claim—at the insurer's instructions—against the express wishes of the insured.

> **Who's in Charge?**
>
> *The insurer has the final say, but the insurance company in a fronted, retrospectively rated, or high deductible program must consider the insured's wishes in its settle or deny-and-defend decisions.*

That said, however, the insurer in a fronted, retrospectively rated, or high deductible policy must take the insured's desires into account in its settle or deny-and-defend decisions. The insured's best interests also must be protected, even in a process as common as setting reserves for a retrospectively rated policy, where the reserves become part of the incurred cost. If the reserves are set unreasonably high, the insured's premium is adversely affected, perhaps unethically. In *Liberty Mutual v. Marty's Express,* 910

F. Supp. 221 (E.D. Pa. 1996), the court stated that the insured must produce enough evidence to suggest that the insurer did not act reasonably and in good faith when handling claims in a retrospectively rated policy. The burden then passes to the insurer, which bears the ultimate responsibility of proving that it did act reasonably and in good faith under such a policy.

The insurer also should take the insured's settlement desires into consideration under such policies. Quite often the claimant in a third-party action may be the insured's customer, business associate (as in a subcontractor situation), or valued employee. If the insurer takes a hard-nosed negotiating position with such a claimant for amounts that fall within the insured's deductible, then the insurer could upset a valuable relationship that insured has cultivated over time.

In addition, the insurer must take positive steps to understand the insured's entire risk management program. Coverage may overlap, excess coverage may be involved, and some claims may be uninsured.

No Insurance versus Self-Insurance

Too many people in the commercial risk industry tend to equate no insurance with self-insurance, but the two arrangements are completely different. Self-insurance should be an actuarially sound program based on a large number of homogeneous exposure units, and, in many cases such as workers compensation or auto financial responsibility, approved by state regulators. Using funds from an approved self-insurance plan or self-funded program to pay noncovered losses erodes the intent of the plan.

These types of mistakes occurred frequently before Employment Practices Liability (EPL) insurance became available. Often employers who were self-insured or self-funded with high deductible policies would direct their third-party claims administrators to handle wrongful termination, discrimination, or harassment claims under the workers compensation program, reasoning that these were alleged injuries to employees. However, the claims did not fall within the scope of the workers compensation laws, the self-insured and state-approved plans, or the National Council on Compensation Insurance, Inc., (NCCI) workers compensation form. As a result of running the costs—including the high defense costs—of such claims through their workers compensation programs, their entities' experience modifiers were increased and data regarding employment injuries and illnesses were distorted.

Churning: Fishing for the Commission

The need to attract new business is a constant in the marketing and production side of insurance. Some of that business will come from current and former clients. Much of it will come from new clients. However, the insurance laws in most jurisdictions specifically proscribe churning or twisting, practices in which a salesperson tries to convince a client to change insurers or purchase inferior coverage at a higher premium in order to make more commission. In Florida, for example, the Medicare supplement insurance industry at one time was notorious for frightening elderly people into purchasing supplemental policies of little real value at costs they could not afford.

When a broker or agent attempts to push an insurance product simply to gain sales and increase commissions, the sales might be considered to be unethical. Many commercial risks, recognizing that commissions are a significant part of insurance premiums, therefore, purchase coverage net of commission and pay the agent or broker an annual fee for services. Even with such agreements, there may be insurers that, because of built-in rating factors, continue to charge for commissions and return them to the agent or broker. If the agent or broker already has been paid a fee, the ethical response would be to return that commission to the insured. There are many in the industry who do not agree, however.

What's Your Position?

Contingency profit arrangements have been criticized by many. Are contingency agreements ethical? Must they be disclosed to clients?

Another insurer-brokerage-insured issue that occasionally becomes an ethical issue is that of contingency profit arrangements, in which a broker or agent—perhaps retained by the insured on a fee contract basis—is monetarily rewarded by an insurer for bringing a profitable book of business to the insurer. Perhaps, suggests Susan Meltzer, a corporate risk manager and former president of the Risk and Insurance Management Society (RIMS), in the April 1998 issue of *Risk Management*, the problem is that the insurance distribution system "was developed primarily to meet the needs of small and midsize organizations and individuals," not the large international corporations of the twenty-first century. For such large commercial entities, insurance is only one of many alternative risk financing tools. The relationship between insurer and insured, with the broker or agent as the party in the middle, is much different than it was in the 1960s.

Mergers: Big Brokers, Little Agents, and Giant Insurers

In the 1970s, national brokerage firms began seeking local affiliates in many cities, merging with or acquiring smaller firms. The basic difference between agents and brokers is representation: a broker represents the insured to the insurance company, while the agent represents the company to the insured. Agents may be independent, representing a number of insurance companies, or captive, representing only a single carrier. By the early 1980s, many in the insurance industry predicted the demise of the independent agency system, at least as far as commercial risks were concerned. They alleged that smaller agencies had neither the capability of representing larger risks nor the clout with insurers that wrote commercial coverage. Time has shown that these predictions were incorrect. The independent agency system is still very much a part of the commercial risk industry.

The insurance business remains highly competitive. Commercial insurers spend billions of dollars annually advertising their companies and services. The agents and brokers likewise advertise and compete in a variety of ways to attract clients. Such advertising and competition is good for the industry and consumers because it presents choices. The elimination of choices does not benefit consumers. Despite this, the top ten brokerage firms of 1990 have been whittled down to the top three firms of 2001. An alphabet soup of brokerage mergers, preceding a number of insurer mergers, eliminated many options for commercial risks.

The issue for many, however, was one of ethics. In the early 1990s, one brokerage firm suggested that its corporate insureds might no longer need risk managers because the brokerage firm could provide risk management services. Many felt this proposal involved a conflict of interest because, by definition, a commercial risk management plan takes into account many forms of risk

> **Do You Agree?**
>
> The elimination of choices does not benefit consumers.

financing and not just insurance products. Since the broker's primary role, unless the firm is working on a contract fee basis rather than a commission basis, is to represent an insured to insurers, potential elimination of competing risk financing procedures may have benefited only the broker and not necessarily the insureds.

There are many advantages to bigness, however, just as there are disadvantages. Size brings with it a greater capacity, an ability to write more hazardous risks, and a firmer financial position in the global marketplace. This expansion, therefore, is a logical, and, on the surface, ethical response to the realities of the twenty-first century.

Thought Provokers

1. A large commercial entity, after realizing that less than 60 percent of its liability premium dollar is spent paying for actual loss, decides that it can do better by *self-insuring* that risk. What factors should be considered before a final decision is made?

2. A commercial entity decides to open its broker/agency agreement to bidding and sends out a Request for Proposal (RFP). The RFP includes a specification that only *ethical* agents and brokers will be considered. What type of criteria might be used to evaluate the ethics of the applicants?

3. A new resident in a small town approaches a local independent agent for coverage on a dwelling he has just purchased. There is no mortgage on the house. The information that he provides to the agent about the house is rather vague and very general. The agent is aware that his underwriters are eager for new business and may not pay too much attention to the application. What ethical steps might the agent take to be certain that the risk is both valid and acceptable?

4. XYZ Corporation is in the process of acquiring the ABC Company, which had recently merged with N&N, Inc. N&N operated a chemical-manufacturing subsidiary, which XYZ also is acquiring. N&N had placed its insurance with a local agent that is located in a state different from either XYZ's or ABC's location. ABC's insurance service is with a regional brokerage firm. XYZ uses a national brokerage firm. What are the ethical duties of each of the three companies and their insurance representatives?

Chapter 4

Good Faith or *Utmost* Good Faith?

"Any of the following acts by an insurer, if committed [as a general business practice], constitutes an unfair claims practice . . .

*D. Not attempting in **good faith** to effectuate prompt, fair and equitable settlement of claims submitted in which liability has become reasonably clear."*

§4. NAIC Model Unfair
Claims Settlement Practice Act

Contracts should be executed in the spirit of good faith and fair dealing. When a party to a contract acts in an unfaithful way or deals unfairly, the contract is breached. Insurance contracts likewise must be entered in good faith and fair dealing. In fact, this requirement may have even greater implications in insurance than in other business areas. Most of those implications are ethical in nature.

Certain criteria must exist in order for the insurance contract to be valid. First there must be *offer and acceptance.* That is the role of marketing or production in regard to the policy. But it is also a key factor in claim settlement. There also must be *legality of purpose.* The party purchasing the insurance must have an insurable interest in the subject of insurance. For example, an individual may not purchase a life insurance policy on a stranger without a financial interest in that person's life. Such a purchase, in fact, might encourage fraud—perhaps even murder. But neither should an insurer issue a contract on which it has little intent of paying claims. As noted in Chapter 3, when that occurs, the industry suffers a serious blow.

Two additional criteria for a valid contract are *consideration* and the *capacity to contract.* Consideration implies an exchange of value. In equity that exchange should be equal. As discussed in Chapter 1, the insurance contract is aleatory in nature, and a policy is only equal to the premium in an actuarial format— what is purchased as a promise based on statistics. If those statistics are invalid— perhaps because of incorrect information— the contract is unethically unequal even though there is consideration.

Criteria for Contracts

Offer and acceptance
Legality of purpose
Consideration
Capacity to contract

The capacity to contract also is significant in the insurance setting. It is close in many ways to legality of purpose, for only those with an insurable interest in the subject of insurance legally have the capacity to enter the contract. While capacity often refers to factors such as age, mental capacity, or legal standing—and those factors are significant in the insurance contract—there are times when minors or incompetents can become insureds if the purpose is legal and, most significantly, if a guardian or other fiduciary acts on their behalf. But capacity works from the other direction as well. The insurer must have the legal standing to market an insurance product. Foreign (nonapproved) insurers can market in states in which they are not specifically approved, but even these situations are covered by state regulations.

Faith to Ethics

Insurance involves good faith contracts, but what is meant by *faith?* Faith can have many meanings. It usually is closely aligned with religion, a word often interchangeable with faith. Perhaps there is a closer relationship between insurance and religion than many twenty-first century insurance practitioners suspect. There always has been a relationship between religion and courts, where those testifying in many jurisdictions place their hands on a Bible and swear to tell the truth "so help me God." Court petitions often are steeped in religious language, such as a "prayer for damages" or an award of *exemplary* damages.

Likewise, the early policies issued at Underwriters at Lloyds in the seventeenth century began, "In the name of God, Amen." Certain perils of nature were—and still are—referred to as "acts of God," as if a Supreme Being caused storms, volcanic eruptions, or earthquakes deliberately.

So what is *faith?* Dictionaries use words such as belief, trust, system of beliefs, rules or laws, standards of behavior, acceptance of certain responsibilities, and affirmations, terms which are not necessarily tangible or scientifically provable. All of these definitions might be applied to the insurance relationship.

But the contractual rule requires that the faith be *good faith.* Good faith cannot be weak, blind, inactive, or bad. To be *good,* faith must be based on correct theories, study, understanding, the building of relationships, and positive actions.

Know the Relationship

There must be complete understanding of the relationships between the insured and insurer—and potential third parties.

The same is true for insurance contracts. There must be a complete understanding of the relationships between the insured and insurer—and potential third parties. That understanding must be active, based on study and knowledge about the involved risks by both the insured and the insurer. The relationship must be personal and positive. The insurance relationship in large part involves belief in things we cannot always see. We cannot see the future, which is when an insurance policy is applicable: future loss, unforeseen, fortuitous. The insured must place considerable trust in the insurer to be there when a covered loss occurs. In an exchange of nothing more than a promise and a stack of printed paper from an insurer, the policyholder may pay hundreds or thousands of dollars. That is an expression of faith on the part of the policyholder.

In exchange the insurer must express its faith in the policyholder. Insurers know that some policyholders will make claims. It must rely on the insurance mechanisms that are in place to make sure those claims are both made and paid in good faith. The insurance company has to trust its policyholders, just as those policyholders must place their faith in the insurer.

Rules of Behavior

What does this discussion of faith and religion have to do with ethics? Actually, it is the key, the very heart of ethics. As noted previously, ethics implies a system of moral behavior. Faith also involves moral behavior. Both represent attitudes and behavior that are much higher than law. Law is the absolute minimum standard of behavior; ethics is the highest standard of behavior.

Ethical behavior must go far beyond the minimum. These standards and precepts are expressed in a key word: *responsibility*. Ethical people take, and accept, responsibility. One nationally known ethics expert, Gary Edward, CPCU, chief executive of the Ethics Resource Center in Washington, D.C., often uses the example of the Tylenol capsule tampering case of the 1980s to

Do You Agree?

Ethical behavior must go far beyond the minimum. These standards and precepts are expressed in a key word: responsibility. Ethical people take, and accept, responsibility.

illustrate an ethical corporate response to a difficult situation. The company had a recall policy in place before the event occurred. Senior corporate officials learned that the procedure was being carried out from the media. This illustrated a *top down* ethical policy resulting in *bottom up* action. Local and regional personnel acted ethically because of a corporate policy; the law did not require it, at least at that time.

Another example is that of Kate Shelley, the wife of a railway lineman on the Chicago & Northwestern Railroad. She did not work for the railroad, and she had no legal obligations to it. Yet on the night of July 6, 1881, she fought her way through a blinding thunderstorm to the depot where an eastbound Chicago express train was about to depart, to stop the train. Hurried businessmen and other anxious passengers aboard the train might have severely criticized this unauthorized woman for stopping the flow of commerce—they had business in Chicago, after all.

But the Shelleys' home was next to the Honey Creek Bridge near the Des Moines River. Because Kate was a responsible, moral, and ethical person who recognized that the storm was causing flooding conditions, she went out in the storm to check the bridge. It was starting to collapse. Knowing that a train was due to cross it, she frantically ran to the depot, saving hundreds of lives from a terrible accident.

Was the railroad upset with Kate Shelley's interference with their operations? Not in the least. For an entire century the C&NW passenger trains were named the *Kate Shelley*. The replacement bridge still is named for Kate, a truly ethical hero.

But faith and ethics have a reverse side as well. Ethics, as Aristotle suggested, often imply conflicts in morality. Opinions differ on many subjects, including morality, and taking responsibility occasionally can result in a negative situation. Many grocery stores place candy and toys at the checkout counter where busy parents must stand in line while their children scream for the candy. Is it ethical for the grocery store to put the candy in the checkout area? Is it ethical for the parent to discipline the child in public? Is it ethical for another patron to accuse that parent of child abuse and have the criminal courts determine their fate? From prosecutor to jury, each participant in these actions act primarily on the basis of their own faith and beliefs, for those are the primary resources for our decision-making processes.

Taking Control or Taking Charge?

There is a difference between taking control and taking charge. That difference has much to do with ethics. A trucker involved in a serious accident on the highway—whether or not it is his fault—has an obligation to take control if he is physically able. He must set out flares, call for aid, and attend to injuries until help arrives. It is the official help—the police, fire department, department of transportation, or EPA—that has the legal authority and is in charge. But the individuals who are involved must be in control. Failure to take control of any situation is a failure to be ethical.

Many describe ethics as it relates to morals. Ethics may be defined as moral obligations. Morals may be a cross between official rules or laws and standards of behavior. An immoral act may or may not be an illegal act, but it generally would be considered an unethical act. Moral decisions are made daily. Some, such as transactions that affect how much we pay in income tax, may be against the law even though committed by moral, upright people. Other acts may not be against the law but are looked upon by society as immoral or improper actions.

What some consider to be unethical or immoral behavior may be considered by others as just good business practice. The business world often is cutthroat, super-competitive, and mean-spirited. Business tactics can be cruel, unfair, demoralizing, and, for the losers, devastating, but entirely legal and, in the eyes of those who profit from the business, righteous and upstanding.

Immoral acts affect another closely related emotion—morale. History suggests that it was over-exuberance and speculation combined with the use of credit that caused the October 1929 stock market crash that led to the Great Depression. The same factors led to a severe market decline in the second half of 2000 for new economy dot.com stocks that had little real value. Like the motto of Alfred E. Newman in *Mad Magazine,* the national emotion seemed to be

> **Who Is Right?**
>
> *What some consider to be unethical or immoral behavior may be considered by others as just good business practice.*

"What, *me* worry?" When things are going well people tend to overextend, fail to take hazards into account, and become complacent. This becomes a morale hazard, and morale hazards are ethical issues.

Medical specialists often suggest that people who allow their anger to build hurt themselves; therefore they should let their anger out. But there is an opposite side to that—the hurt to those upon whom that anger is unleashed. Uncontrolled outbursts of anger toward others, in the form of office rage, road rage, or sports rage, are unacceptable both ethically and morally. Methods to deal with such frustrations intertwine with ethics. A person who takes on too many activities and then becomes frustrated and angry because he is unable to do them all may be just as unethical as the person who shuns the responsibility of any activities. Some businesses pile too much on their employees because they won't hire enough personnel; and then they fail to properly equip and educate that staff, constantly threatening downsizing to the point that the stress becomes overwhelming. They may be acting immorally and unethically, although perfectly legally.

Cover-up

The antithesis of ethical behavior is a cover-up. This has been evident in the downfall of people for centuries, from our presidents to coworkers and neighbors. Often the original misdeed is of minor consequence compared with the trouble that results from the attempt to hide it. Most of us learned the hazards of a cover-up as children. We would sweep the pieces of broken crockery under the rug, hoping that the evidence would disappear. It never did! We would fib about who was responsible and the punishment for the lie would be far worse than the original transgression. When untrue and misleading testimony is given under oath in a court of law, it is called perjury and is punishable by fines and imprisonment. It fails to meet not only the minimum legal standard but also the ethical standard. Perhaps it is this unethical desire to deny responsibility and cover up the facts that make it so difficult to find reliable witnesses to crimes and loss. People simply do not want to be involved.

> **Cover-up Issues**
>
> *Cover-up, denial, and misleading statements play a significant role in unethical business practices.*

Cover-up, denial, and misleading statements play a significant role in unethical business practices as well. When something goes wrong, there is inevitably a lot of finger pointing, excuses, and spin control that does little to win respect for the industry. For example, it came to light in the year 2000 that more than a hundred people had been killed and hundreds permanently injured in accidents involving sport utility vehicles (SUVs) and tire tread separation problems. The vehicle manufacturer pointed the finger at the tire manufacturer, which pointed it back at the SUV manufacturer. But nobody pointed it at one possibly culpable party in the scenario—the insurance industry. If all those accidents had been occurring for years, why had no one in the industry noticed? Was no one gathering information any more? Since the industry was involved in every aspect of the claims involving those vehicles and those tires, it was in a prime position to take control, to seek out some authority that would take charge. Instead, one company, even though it had begun to recognize the hazardous tire-SUV problem, decided to lower the premium rate for SUVs. It was all quite legal. But law is the minimum standard. Ethics is the highest.

In a biographical review of Robert D. Krebs, a very successful railroad executive, Fred W. Failey describes Krebs' reputation for having a bad temper. According to Failey, Krebs learned that his temper could cause a negative by-product, a cover-up, when he was trying to combine two railroads into a single successful operation. "People had become scared of Krebs," writes Frailey, "to the point that some wouldn't give him honest feedback." Intimidation that leads to this type of cover-up is bad for an operation. Failure to provide honest responses to a situation may develop into an unethical cover-up.

Understanding Good Faith and Fair Dealing

Most courts have ruled that an insurer owes a good faith duty only to its own insured. The duty exists because of the contractual relationship and should apply primarily between the insurer and the policyholder.

However, courts have ruled in a number of states that insurers also owe a good faith duty to third-party claimants. Some of these decisions are based on the states' unfair claims settlement practices acts, while others are based on legislation such as consumer fraud or deceptive and unfair trade-practices laws. These rulings may create ethical dilemmas because the third-party claimant is not a party to the insurance contract.

For example, in Kentucky, third-party claimants are permitted to bring independent actions against insurers for violation of the state's Unfair Claims Settlement Practices Act *(State Farm Mutual Automobile Insurance Company v. Reeder,* 763 S.W.2d 116 [Ky. 1988]). In West

Virginia, such a right of action arose out of *Hayseeds, Inc. v. State Farm Fire & Casualty Co.,* 352 S.E.2d 73 (W. Va. 1986). Although a first-party claim, *Hayseeds* led to a right of action by third-party claimants, as seen in the later *Dodrill v. Nationwide Mutual Ins. Co.,* 491 S.E.2d 1 (W. Va. 1996). In *Dodrill,* the West Virginia Supreme Court focused on the part of the act requiring settlement in good faith fairly, promptly, and equitably whenever liability was reasonably clear. The insurer had handled the claim by phone from another state prior to the litigation and used several different adjusters, none of who ever saw pictures of the claimant's damaged auto. However, the Court failed to explain its decision that the insurer had acted in less than good faith and focused more on the definition of "a general business practice," one requirement for a claim under the Act.

Other courts have extended, at least in part, a right of action to parties who are not policyholders. The first such cases were in the late 1970s in California, under *Royal Globe v. Superior Court,* 153 Cal. Rptr. 843 (1979). Within ten years that decision had caused so much litigation that a later state Supreme Court reversed it in *Moradi-Shalal v. Fireman's Fund,* 226 Cal. Rptr. 333 (1988). Montana also issued a similar ruling in *Klaudt v. Flink,* 658 P.2d 414 (1986), but the court reversed itself in that state due to the chaos the ruling created. Other states that permit third-party actions include Massachusetts, under the state's Unfair & Deceptive Trade Practices Act §93-1 and §176-D, and Texas, under the state's Deceptive Trade Practices - Consumer Protection Act §17.001-.45, both of which permit treble damages.

A state-by-state analysis of how courts approach a noncontractual relationship in terms of good faith and fair dealing demonstrates shifts back and forth on the issue of third-party rights of action against insurers. Most states, however, continue to hold that such a duty exists only between an insured and insurer.

There are thousands of first-party bad faith claims, most arising out of insurers' interpretation of their own coverage or disputes over valuation. Not all states agree, however, that a right of action exists for first-party bad faith. Some cases in which such actions were allowed involve allegations of bad faith cancellation of coverage, refusal to renew, or rescission. Another cause of action may arise out of an insurer's inability to prove fraud or arson against its policyholder, as seen in the Ohio case of *Wagoner v. Midwestern Indem. Co.,* 699 N.E.2d 507 (1998). In that case the court reinstated an $800,000

punitive damage award against the insurer that unsuccessfully de-
fended a claim on the basis of suspected arson. Bad faith claims under
an Unfair Claims Settlement Practice Act may involve damage issues.
In *Farmland Mutl. Ins. Co. v. Johnson* (an unpublished Kentucky court
decision in 1998), the issue was the definition of actual cash value. The
case involved an allegation that the agent had misrepresented policy
language. In the Ohio case of *Greenberg v. Life Ins. Co. of Va.*, 177 F.3d
507 (6th Cir. 1999), the issue involved marketing comments by the
insurer's agent that were contrary to policy terminology. Many first-
party bad faith claims arise out of life and health insurance policies,
although a number of these are subject to federal jurisdiction under
ERISA.

However, the bulk of insureds' claims of bad faith against insurers
arise from failure to protect the insured's interests in a third-party
action. The ethical issue, however, is not solely one of good faith/bad
faith or violation of unfair and deceptive trade practice legislation.
Analysis of those cases shows that a fair dealing issue lies at the heart
of many such claims, primarily one of *disclosure*. Insurers and their
representatives may get into trouble if they fail to recognize their duty
to disclose all the information that relates to a claim. The claim adjuster
or attorney must balance the insurer's role in providing peace of mind
with the realities of a serious third-party action, such as in cases in
which a court may award a plaintiff more than the coverage provides.
That failure to keep the insured informed, and failure to allow her to
participate in the decision-making processes, is at the root of most bad
faith claims.

The late Pat Magarick cited a 1933 New York case, *Kirke La Shelle
Co. v. Paul Armstrong Co.*, 188 N.E. 163 (1933), as having great impact
on the subject of bad faith. The court in that case said that "in every
contract there is an implied covenant that neither party shall do
anything which will have the effect of destroying or injuring the right
of the other party to receive the fruits of the contract, which means that
in every contract there exists an implied covenant of good faith and
fair dealing." Third-party bad faith cases have arisen out of any number
of factors relating to the defense and settlement of claims against the
insured. They involve not only coverage and limits of liability issues,
but also improper investigation, improper evaluation, improper defense or negotiation, refusal to defend a party entitled to coverage
under the policy, and similar issues. It generally is not enough for the

insured to demonstrate that a bad result occurred, nor even that the insurer's negligence caused that result, but that the insurer knew or should have known that its negligent action would cause a bad result.

One historic problem in the insurance industry has been its reluctance to provide full and complete information about its coverage, its claim processes, and its settlement decisions. Insurance policies traditionally relied on fine print, with conditions and exclusions printed in such small type as to be almost unreadable. Only when the courts began to frown on this did insurers revise their approach and, beginning in the 1970s, switch to what is called lucid language policy forms in which the insured is referred to as "you", and the company as "we". Yet, even with the more easily understood policy forms, the language, conditions and exclusions, and exceptions to exclusions continue to generate litigation. Not only the words, but the intent and meaning of the words, must be disclosed.

Insurer Duties

An insurer has a duty to be up front with policyholders about what is and is not covered and to keep them *fully* informed about what is happening on their claims. Failure to comply with these two requirements accounts for the bulk of insurance-related litigation.

Disclosure means many things. An insurer has a duty to be up front with policyholders about what is and is not covered and to keep them *fully* informed about what is happening on their claims. Failure to comply with these two requirements accounts for the bulk of insurance-related litigation.

Fully explaining fair dealing as it is interpreted across the nation could take volumes. *Fair* is a subjective term, and each party's viewpoint in a dealing determines what is fair. Deceptive trade-practice laws and unfair claims acts establish rock-bottom minimum standards of behavior. Ethics establishes the maximum standard. So, what should that standard be?

One of the key words in the NAIC Model Unfair Claims Settlement Act is "equitable." A dictionary might list fair as its synonym, but that creates a circle. *Webster's New World College Dictionary* (1984) defines the law of equity as a "resort to general principles of fairness and justice whenever existing law is inadequate; a system of rules and doctrines, such as in the U.S., supplementing common and statutory law when it proves inadequate for just settlement; a right or claim recognized in a court of equity, [and] same as equity of redemption."

This is less than helpful in defining either fair or equitable, however. A better analysis may be in the root word, *aequi*, which means even. To be fair or equitable, a contract must be *even* between the parties. This is implied in the word *indemnification*, one of the keys to ethics in insurance. A policy of insurance must be even in its offers and acceptances, its intents and purposes, and its considerations, despite the fact that it is aleatory. That evenness comes from accurate statistical data and information about the individual risk that result in an accurate premium. It also is represented in accurate information about the loss and what is and is not covered. Errors either way—underpaying or overpaying a claim—defeat equitableness. Such dealing, therefore, becomes unfair, and the objective of the insurance contract is breached.

Bona Fide or Uberrimae Fidei?

In a presentation at the *Claims Magazine's* 2000 Claims Exposition and Conference, Bruce Hillman, managing editor of *FC&S Bulletins*, (National Underwriter Co.) discussed bad faith claims. He said that an insurer's duty was higher than just good faith. Insurance contracts may require *Bona Fide* or *uberrimae fidei*—ultimate or utmost good faith. That implies the highest degree of trust on the part of both the insured and the insurer.

Utmost good faith requires more than just positive belief and responsible action. It implies being totally above reproach, acting at the highest moral and ethical standard. This attitude of duty must permeate the entire insuring organization if the objective is to be obtained. There first must be a sense of loyalty between the insurer and its own employees, an attitude that may seem lacking in twenty-first century business relationships. That loyalty or sense of duty must extend outward in all directions, from the marketers to the adjusters. If a sense of duty and loyalty between the insurer and its policyholders is lacking, utmost good faith may not exist, even though the relationship is legal and proper.

This carries over as well to those who are not directly employed by the insurer but act on its behalf as agents, brokers, independent adjusters, or defense attorneys. These persons must meet just as high a degree of trust and loyalty as direct employees.

It is the utmost good faith requirement that separates—or should separate—the insurance industry from other businesses. Its product is protection, peace of mind, being there when the catastrophe occurs, and being financially strong enough to pay its claims and remain in business. That is more than required of other types of business. It constitutes the utmost in faith.

Is There a Fiduciary Relationship?

There is considerable debate within the insurance industry and the courts about whether insurance involves a *fiduciary* relationship. Fiduciary is primarily a legal term that means one who acts on behalf of another in a matter of trust, usually in an utmost good faith relationship. It implies much more than just an *agency* relationship. Common fiduciaries include executors or administrators of estates, trustees, bankruptcy receivers, guardians—individuals or entities appointed to act in the ultimate best interests of another. Politicians are technically fiduciaries because they act on behalf of and for the public's best interest. The courts often require a bond from such appointees; these bonds respond if the fiduciary acts with misfeasance, malfeasance, or nonfeasance.

Many insurance legal experts resist the suggestion that insurance is a fiduciary relationship and that its representatives are fiduciaries. They argue that the relationship is simply one of agency. The reasons for dispute reflect ethical issues. A fiduciary is held to a very high degree of care; he must demonstrate utmost good faith in every act. All actions must be in the best interest of those involved. That places a much higher degree of responsibility on such individuals than does a nonfiduciary relationship. A salesman may represent a product manufacturer but does not act as a fiduciary for that manufacturer. But insurance is a unique product. It is intangible until loss occurs.

There is logic behind the argument that a first-party relationship between the insurer and the policyholder is *not* a fiduciary one. In *Bailey v. Allstate Ins. Co.,* 844 P.2d 1336 (Colo. App.1992), the court found that an insurer does not have a true fiduciary relationship with its insured because the interests of the two parties are considered equal. That may be true unless the insurer attempts to take over the insured's loss by requiring the insured to use *only* authorized repair or replacement facilities, a specific physician or medical service—or *only* treatment approved by the insurer. However, if the insurer steps into a role beyond that established by the policy contract, it may become a fiduciary.

The situation, however, changes in a third-party action. Absent a consent-to-settle clause, a liability policy gives the insurer—not the insured—the right and duty to settle or defend as *it* deems appropriate. This imposes a responsibility on insurers to settle or defend a claim whenever coverage applies, to the limits of its liability, on behalf of an insured who may not necessarily be the policyholder, especially in cases of additional insureds. Therein lies a significant difference. The insurer "acts on behalf of" the insured in a position of trust under most liability forms.

California's courts have ruled both ways. In *Gruenberg v. Aetna Ins. Co.*, 9 Cal. 3d 566 (1973), the court suggests that there is no fiduciary duty imposed on an independent adjuster who is not a party to the contract. Other California cases have also held that there is no fiduciary duty between an insured and insurer. However, a California court ruled that a fiduciary relationship did exist in the case of *Frommoethelydo v. Fire Ins. Exch.*, 721 P. 2d 41 (Cal. 1986). Not all courts, nor certainly all insurance experts, agree.

In *Rector v. Husted*, 519 P.2d 634 (Kan. 1974), a Kansas court ruled that an insurer has a fiduciary duty to look after the interests of its insured when evaluating a settlement offer that falls within the policy limits. In similar fashion, the Seventh Circuit ruled that failure of an insurer to inform its insured about offers to settle within the policy limits was a bad faith breach of the insurer's *fiduciary* relationship. (*Bailey v. Prudence Mutual Cas. Co.*, 429 F.2d 1388 [7th Cir. 1970]). Other decisions that include a recognition of the insurance relationship as fiduciary in nature include *Gibson v. Geico*, 162 Cal. App. 3d 441 (1984); *Nat'l Farmers Union P&C Co. v. O'Daniel*, 329 F.2d 60 (9th Cir. 1964); and *Lieberman v. Employers Ins.*, 419 A.2d 417 (N.J. 1980).

Attitudes change. One textbook used for the Insurance Institute of America's Associate in Claims programs in the 1960s was *Casualty Insurance Claims* (Irwin Press). In it, author James Donaldson, LL.B., states "the claims representative is a fiduciary agent." However, the Fifth Edition of that same text, coauthored by the Defense Research Institute's Donald Hirsch, J.D., removed the fiduciary agent language, replacing it with the phrase "special trust and confidence." Is that phrase the same, legally, as the term fiduciary? An argument could be made either way. As Aristotle suggested, ethics implies moral dilemmas.

Faith versus Fraud

According to the I.I.I., property and casualty insurance industry estimates that it lost $21 billion in 1998 to fraud. The I.I.I. suggests that fraud losses may be as high as $120 billion, or $1,000 per family that purchases insurance. In auto insurance, the industry estimates that 20 percent of the *claim dollar* is lost to fraud. Considering that the claim dollar represents only about 60 percent of the premium dollar, roughly twelve cents of every dollar in premium is fraudulent. Since as much as 40 percent of the claim dollar is used for legal expenses, as little as twenty-four cents of each dollar in premium is used to pay legitimate claims—not a very balanced return.

How Serious?

The insurance industry believes it has a serious fraud problem.

Such estimates, of course, are factored into premium rates, which include provisions for the insurer's intended profit. The cost of fighting fraud also may be included in those cost-of-fraud figures.

What is clear is that the insurance industry believes it has a serious fraud problem. Fraud costs are undoubtedly discussed whenever premium rate increase approval is sought. Many states have begun to require that insurers address fraud, and the result has been increased spending on fraud investigation, usually in the form of special investigation units (SIU). Such units, often staffed by former police detectives, federal agents, private investigators, or others familiar with white-collar crime, are assigned cases when a fraudulent situation is suspected. Their actions and investigations undoubtedly help to prevent fraud, although the conviction rate for insurance fraud remains very low.

Actual Fraud Is Hard to Prove

One dilemma is that the insurance industry cannot prove that it is losing all those billions of dollars to fraud. The I.I.I. statistics are based on two categories of crime: hard and soft fraud. Hard fraud includes deliberate criminal actions such as staged accidents, padded bills, false testimony, auto theft rings, arson for profit, staged burglaries, and similar crimes. For example, physicians may submit false medical bills to insurers for services they did not provide.

Soft fraud, even SIU proponents admit, is harder to prove, although there is some indication that the industry sees it as the source of major source of fraud loss. Soft fraud includes acts such as exaggerating real injury symptoms, malingering or failing to return to gainful activity after a reasonable period of disability, creating factitious disorders for psychological reasons, overstating values in property losses, or claiming the loss of items that were not owned. Insurers can cite industry studies in which large percentages of people admit that they would exaggerate a claim to cover a deductible or to recoup at least the amount of their premium. National trends in attitudes toward institutions have deteriorated, and many people have no inhibition about exaggerating claims.

Who or what is to blame for this tremendous alleged loss? One possible answer is that there has been moral decay in our national ethical standards. But that is not necessarily the correct answer, nor is it an ethically acceptable answer for the insurance industry to adopt. The true fact—hard as it may be for many SIU proponents to believe—is that the majority of Americans are scrupulously honest and do not cheat, lie, or exaggerate their claims. Most have no desire to even make a claim.

Perhaps a better answer lies in the facts related in Chapters 1 and 3, about the evolution of the industry and the resulting impersonal relationship between insurers and insureds. There is little to prevent what the industry alleges as major fraud losses when coverage can be purchased online, over the telephone, or by mail with no direct contact between agent and policyholder, and when both first- and third-party claims are handled by phone and mail. How much of the $21 billion dollars in alleged fraud losses might be saved if the insurance industry invested more in outside claims adjusting service? If the issue is ethics, these types of questions must be addressed.

Perhaps another look at the problem is needed. As noted previously, *faith* must include many factors, from trust and belief to understanding and the establishment of a positive, active relationship.

Can the insurance industry ethically justify premiums that include factors for fraud loss while their lack of faith in the policyholder or the third-party claimant suggests he is a crook? Some SIU advocates seem to imply that anyone with the audacity to make a claim must have an illegal intent. Sometimes it seems as if insurance thieves are everywhere. But claim adjusters, who by their personal contacts and investigations might prevent such fraud, are nowhere in sight.

Consider, for example, arson for profit, a crime that existed well before that day in 64 A.D. when Nero performed while Rome burned. Insurers spend millions of dollars every year on arson investigations attempting to prove that the insured did it. Federal Bureau of Investigation statistics show that only a relatively small percentage of arson fires is for profit. However, more than 50 percent of such fires are caused by juveniles, quite often children who start the fires for psychological reasons. The amount spent by the insurance industry to prevent juvenile arson compared to what is spent investigating arson for profit is not known, but the relative amounts probably are not in proportion to the actual causes.

> **Do You Agree?**
>
> *One aspect of ethics is balance. Balance must be achieved by an insurance industry that acts in utmost good faith and establishes trusting relationships with its policyholders in order to operate ethically.*

One aspect of ethics is *balance*. It is implied in the terms discussed previously, including equitable and indemnity. Whenever any industry gets out of balance it becomes unethical. Balance must be achieved by an insurance industry that acts in utmost good faith and establishes trusting relationships with its policyholders in order to operate ethically.

Corporate and Individual Integrity

Accidents do not simply happen. They may be unintended and fortuitous, but every accident has causes, a collection of hazards that results in a peril. Floods? Windstorms? Forest fires? The hazard simply may be one of location. Commercial risk managers must seek out those hazards and eliminate or treat them to reduce the exposures they create. Likewise it is the role of the parent or the head of a household to seek out hazards and deal with them effectively and morally. Failure to do so is a failure to be responsible. It allows the morale hazard to exist, to eat away at the wholeness of the entity or the family. It creates a lack of integrity and therefore is unethical.

Evidence of a lack of ethical behavior by corporations, governments, and individuals fills the history books. Consider, for example, the steel mill strikes in the late nineteenth century in Pittsburgh. Working conditions in the mills were extremely dangerous; men risked their lives daily for pennies. If the workers complained, they were fired and replaced by another of the jobless immigrants begging for work. When the employees at the Homestead Carnegie Steel plant staged a lockout strike in 1892, Andrew Carnegie's associate, Henry Clay Frick, brought in Pinkerton agents, and a massacre resulted.

Society Responsible

No one person, no one sex, no single race or religion has a lock on ethics. It is society itself that must strive for integrity in its corporations, governments, institutions, and in each individual home.

Riots and revolutions are part of the American heritage. It is likely that terrorism will replace much of that tradition in the twenty-first century, as groups and individuals respond to inequities and unethical behavior in society with criminal acts. This will result from two issues of ethics: imbalance between the haves and have-nots and lack of personal and corporate integrity, or wholeness.

No one person, no one sex, no single race or religion has a lock on ethics. It is society itself that must strive for integrity in its corporations, governments, institutions, and in each individual home.

Privacy in the Information Age

Few ethical issues will garner as much attention in the twenty-first century as that of privacy. With the rise of the Internet in the final decade of the twentieth century and growing concern over the availability of medical information on individuals, it quickly became evident that complete strangers could access information about private citizens. Privacy of information has become a national issue.

Television ads tout dot.com addresses for criminal background checks on friends, neighbors, or employees. Considering that negligent hiring is a common tort allegation, quick access to criminal records might help

Importance of Privacy

Privacy of information has become a national issue.

employers screen hazardous applicants. The genome directory may result in a databank of the DNA and genes of every American. That may lead to early recognition of diseases and result in many cures.

But there is a potential adverse effect for every positive aspect of such super-scientific advances and technological breakthroughs. Criminal records are not always accurate, and similarities of names often can lead to mistakes. A stolen wallet may mean a stolen identity, and use of a false identity is certainly not new in criminal annals.

Likewise, access to DNA databanks by employers and health insurers might be a wonderful means to screen potentially unhealthy workers or policyholders. That might make for good underwriting but would defeat the primary purpose of insurance, which is to spread the risk.

In 1890, barely a century after the United States Constitution was written, Samuel Warren and Louis Brandeis wrote that "the right to be left alone" was of the utmost importance. The Fourth Amendment to the Constitution protects "The right of the people to be secure in their person, houses, papers and effects, against unreasonable search and seizures . . ." Does the Internet or a medical databank violate that security guarantee? If the government, by virtue of the Bill of Rights, is prohibited from invading our "person, house [or] papers and effects," why should private corporations have the right?

There are a number of state and federal privacy laws already in existence, and more are on the way. These often relate to specific areas of privacy, such as financial credit. However, between these laws and various court decisions there are many gaps. For example, in *California Bankers Association v. Shultz,* 416 U.S. 21 (1974), the Supreme Court held that a bank's record-keeping requirements did not violate the Fourth Amendment right to privacy and did not amount to an illegal search and seizure. The Court, in *United States v. Miller,* 425 U.S. 435 (1976), held that a criminal defendant had no Fourth Amendment right to protection of his bank records and did not have a legitimate expectation of privacy regarding those papers. Attorney R. Mark Bortner, J.D., wrote in1996 that "Concluding over two centuries of Constitutional erosion, it is apparent that an individual's right to financial privacy is limited." His article went on to explain how financial transactions can now be hidden through use of international Internet transactions, thus avoiding the creation of traceable bank records.

Congress, on occasion, attempts to fill these gaps, passing bills such as the *Privacy Act of 1974,* the *Financial Privacy Act of 1982,* and the *Electronic Communications Privacy Act of 1986.*

Other aspects of the privacy issue, besides access to information in cyberspace, affect the ethics of the insurance industry. As discussed previously, the insurance industry spends millions of dollars each year investigating possible fraud. It often uses surveillance and other detection procedures to spy on those who make a claim against an insurer or its policyholder. Does such activity violate an individual's right of privacy? Is it unethical?

The answer lies in our discussion of faith in the first part of this chapter. Faith often involves belief in things we cannot see. But good faith is quite different from blind faith. Good faith is based on study, research, and investigation. The duty of an insurer is to be fair; there is no duty to be naïve.

While there may be a right to be left alone, that right is diminished when individuals open themselves to a claim either through a contract or in tort. The court in one Georgia case commented, "The right of privacy may be implicitly waived, and is waived by one who files an action for injuries from a tort to the extent of the defendant's intervening right to investigate and ascertain for himself the true state of the injury. However, this includes only a waiver of that reasonably unobtrusive type of investigation which would be to the best interests of the defendant in preparing its case." (*Pinkerton National Detective Agency v. Stevens,* 132 S.E.2d 119 [Ga. App. 1963].) While the court found that the detectives had exceeded that extent and were guilty of harassing the plaintiff, the right to investigate has been upheld by most courts.

In *Forster v. Manchester,* 189 A.2d 147 (Pa. 1963), the court summarized what might be unobtrusive in finding that the taking of motion pictures or placing the claimant under surveillance was not an invasion of privacy. However, other courts have found that the use of electronic eavesdropping or wiretapping is invasive and intrusive and therefore an unreasonable aspect of investigation. (*McDaniel v. Atlanta Coca-Cola Bottling Co.,* 2 S.E.2d 810 [Ga. App. 1939].)

Recent mergers between insurance companies, banks, and security investment firms have created new issues of privacy. Can one arm of a corporation, such as a bank, provide free access to its records to another arm, such as insurance? This is a twenty-first century ethical issue; the National Association of Insurance Commissioners has drawn up model legislation for states to consider. The answer, again, is likely to be one relating to balance, for there could be significant benefits as well as risks in such shared information.

Thought Provokers

1. Both an "agent" and a "fiduciary" act on behalf of another. What are the major differences between these two types of legal representatives?

2. A liability insurer, by virtue of its policy contract, has a right and duty to settle or defend covered claims against its insured, to the extent of its limits of liability. If the insurer elects to defend, it may retain the services of an outside defense counsel. Who is the client in such a situation—the insurer or the defendant insured? What role does a good faith duty play in such a relationship?

3. What is the difference between simple good faith and utmost good faith?

4. Can a good faith relationship be established when there is no personal contact between the parties involved in that relationship?

5. An insurance claims representative believes that a man who claims to have been injured in his employment and is represented by an attorney actually is not injured and may be working elsewhere while collecting workers compensation benefits. The claims representative retains an investigator to check on the claimant. What may the investigator ethically do to determine the claimant's status?

Chapter 5

Marketplace Ethics: Buy Low, Sell High

"...I shall strive at all times to live by the highest standards of professional conduct; I shall strive to ascertain and understand the needs of others and place their interests above my own; and I shall strive to maintain and uphold a standard of honor and integrity ..."

CPCU Professional Commitment

The rule of survival in capitalism is "buy low, sell high." When that rule gets out of balance and a person pays more for a product than it ultimately is worth (buying high), the result must be loss. On the other hand, if a service or product is sold at too low a price, it likewise produces loss. In the marketplace, absent some form of governmental tampering, buying and selling prices tend to fall into relative balance. An imbalance—such as may happen in the stock market when over-exuberance results in purchases at too high a price with a decline that forces selling at too low a price—there is severe loss. It therefore falls to the entrepreneur to be certain that an ethical balance in pricing is maintained.

The Right Product, The Right Price

Insurance coverage often is referred to as a *product*, even though it is not manufactured and sold like soap or cars. It also is a service, but it is much more than that. It is a promise or peace of mind; it is having the financial strength to help customers survive loss. But, like soap or cars, insurance is marketed on a pick-and-choose basis.

Hundreds of types of insurance coverages are available. Insurance for some needs is not available, and recognition of those needs usually leads to new types of coverage. Very few individuals who deal in insurance have a good working knowledge of all available products. Life and health agents or brokers often are unfamiliar with property and casualty issues, and vice versa, because people tend to specialize. Personal lines. Commercial lines. Employee benefits. Liability. Property. Surety. Aviation. Marine. The list could fill pages.

A Dilemma

How, then, is an agent or broker to ethically help his or her customer select the right coverage in the correct amounts? It is not easy. Few customers understand their risk and insurance needs.

How, then, is an agent or broker to ethically help his or her customer select the right coverage in the correct amounts? It is not easy. Other than large commercial entities with professional risk managers, few customers understand their risk and insurance needs.

The key to many of these dilemmas is the definition of faith as discussed in the previous chapter: understanding must arise from personal and active relationships. In order to achieve good faith and fair dealing, the paramount objective must be to find a product that fits the customer's needs as precisely as possible.

An acquaintance was involved in an auto accident caused by an uninsured motorist. When she submitted a claim to her agent it was declined because she did not have either first-party collision coverage or uninsured motorists property damage coverage. Both were available. However, she did not understand uninsured motorists coverage, and it was obvious that no one had bothered to explain it to her. She had purchased her insurance solely on price and a need to comply with mandatory insurance laws.

When a policy is first purchased, a customer who does not want to buy uninsured motorists coverage must sign a formal rejection. The law provides that the rejection may be applied to future renewals of that policy. This woman had signed an UM rejection form eight years before the accident. However, between signing the rejection and the accident, she had purchased a different car and obtained coverage with a different insurer through the same agent. There was no subsequent signed formal rejection.

There is a legal issue here: did the rejection signed eight years earlier apply to a new policy from a different carrier that replaced the first? The courts may have to determine that. However, a greater ethical issue is apparent—the need for good faith and fair dealing in the form of understanding and an active personal relationship.

What Do You Think?

Does an agent or broker have a legal obligation to inquire into his customer's lifestyle to determine what risks exist and whether insurance is a way to address them?

Does an agent or broker have a legal obligation to inquire into his customer's lifestyle to determine what risks exist and whether insurance is a way to address them? Court cases go both ways; most hold that the agent is guilty of an error or omission only when a specific request for coverage has not been met. Few courts impose the duty of risk diagnosis. Unless the customer is paying the agent or broker a fee to manage the risks, there may be no such legal obligation.

But is there an ethical duty? The law is the minimum standard. Ethical behavior is the highest standard. To suggest that an agent or broker has no duty to inquire beyond what the customer requests would seem ludicrous to any good businessperson. The questioning has to be something more substantial than, "Is there anything else I can do for you today?" How can typical customers know what products they may need? Insurance marketing should not mimic an old-fashioned grocery store where the customer hands the clerk a list to fill. Marketing should be more like a department store in which customers can browse and see the merchandise, with the clerk offering suggestions. Available coverage must be explained to the customer after the agent or broker learns details about the customer's lifestyle and exposures.

Quantity and Quality

As with any product, price is usually associated with two factors: quantity and quality. The same is true of insurance, with one slight variation. In terms of quantity, it is the lowest levels of coverage that are the most expensive, for those layers of protection will be used first. As more protection is added, especially in liability coverage, the layers become less expensive. They are used less often. Some customers only can *afford* the lowest level of coverage, the minimum amount required. Others, because of their status, driving record, age, or other factors, can *qualify* only for the lowest level of protection, perhaps through an assigned risk pool. Regardless, needs other than price should be discussed with all customers.

Typical discussion items should include determining why a customer buys only limited protection. If the sole reason is cost, exploration of the situation might reveal a severe credit problem. Would referring such a person for credit counseling be an unethical or ethical response by the agent?

Age may be the factor that limits choices. Insurers often provide discounts for students who maintain good grades or take a driver-education class. Does an agent ever have an obligation to discuss driver responsibilities with youthful customers?

> **Number One Concern**
>
> *The number one desire of insureds, according to several industry polls, is fast claims service.*

There comes a time in the lives of many elderly drivers when the family must decide whether to take away "Pop's" or "Granny's" car keys. Anyone who has resided in a retirement community is aware of the daily bangs and crashes involving drivers who have become a menace due to their diminishing faculties. Surprisingly, it is rarely the police or the courts that take away driving privileges. But, as we continually note, the law provides only a minimum standard. Ethical behavior demands the highest standard. Could the standard be to tell the careless teenager or the feeble retiree to use public transportation and forego the sale of expensive coverage that probably is going to result in payment of claims over the policy period?

Other quantity issues should be considered. More commission may be earned when a policyholder lowers a first-party deductible. However, if the customer is financially stable, there can be substantial premium savings with a higher deductible. When the deductible becomes too low, dollar swapping arises. It may be a perfectly legal and accepted practice, but is it ethical?

Quality issues also involve many factors of ethical decision-making. Price often reflects the intended degree of service that is expected. The number one desire of insureds, according to several industry polls, is fast claims service. Many individuals report that their decision to retain an attorney or other representative to act on their behalf was made in an effort to speed up the process. As reported by the Insurance Research Council, however, this is not the case. In general, claims of represented parties take longer to settle, with often lower net recoveries to the claimant, than claims of unrepresented parties.

Quality through Reputation

Some insurers are known for quick and accurate claim settlements. Conversely, others have a reputation for dragging settlements out, negotiating through intimidation, and dealing in practices that might be considered less than full faith and fair dealing—activities that hardly would be considered quality claim service. This may be especially true in third-party claims, which may not directly affect the policyholder unless the third party is an employee, neighbor, or customer. However, delaying settlements may adversely affect the policyholder who is sued because of the delay. It is wise to remember that one benefit of insurance is peace of mind.

Quality also may be reflected in the types of coverage purchased. For example, replacement cost coverage for personal property insurance is more expensive than actual cash value coverage; the difference between them is a quality factor. An agent or broker concerned with providing quality coverage also will explore the need for special endorsements and related coverage with customers. After all, the customers' assets are being protected. If customers consider those assets to have value, the quality of that value must be examined and protected.

> **Do You Agree?**
>
> The ethical agent or broker is not just a supermarket checkout clerk, ringing up sales by scanning bar codes or weighing apples.

In short, the ethical agent or broker is not just a supermarket checkout clerk, ringing up sales by scanning bar codes or weighing apples. He must analyze the lifestyle and coverage needs of each customer individually and act on those factors accordingly. The ultimate selection is, of course, up to the customer, who should be given the tools to make informed decisions. No law requires that this be done, but it is the ethical thing to do. It also can be a very profitable business practice.

Paying the Right Price: Equitable Settlements

In Lewis Carroll's *Through the Looking-Glass,* Alice exclaimed, "I can't believe *that!*" The White Queen replied, "Why, my dear, I make it a point to believe at least five unbelievable things before breakfast each day!"

There are unbelievable things that can be said about the insurance industry in the twenty-first century. But good faith often involves belief in things we cannot prove. There are many in the industry, for example, who cannot believe that the majority of people—including insureds and claimants—are honest. Another unbelievable element of insurance settlements is that the correct amount usually is paid.

Unbelievable?

Good faith often involves belief in things we cannot prove.

How can we be certain that most settlements are correct? As noted previously, claims do not come with bar codes attached. Each is individual and unique, especially to the person making the claim. Claim settlements are negotiated. There are offer and demand, counter-offer and counter-demand, back and forth until agreement is reached. The goal should be to pay the right price for a claim. That, too, is part of the character of the marketplace.

Obviously there are claims where there is little or no negotiation. A policy may specify a limit or maximum payment, and that may be the settlement. Other claims may involve paying a bill or replacing a damaged item. The bulk of claim negotiation occurs, however, when intangibles are involved.

Unequal and Unbalanced

Claim settlement negotiations may be unethical, however, when the parties are unequal and out of balance or when one side attempts to intimidate the other. Insureds and claimants may assume that the adjuster making an offer has superior knowledge of the values involved. That is not always the case. In fact, it may be a widespread misunderstanding. Many claim adjusters and attorneys have as little understanding of claim values as other individuals.

Likewise, the insured or claimant to whom an offer is made—or from whom a demand is solicited—also may have little understanding of the values. They may be intimidated by the process and may speak out of shyness or fear. Many desire only adequate compensation but are not sure what that involves.

Some claim adjusters may try to intimidate claimants into settling for less than a realistic value, and some claimants may attempt to intimidate adjusters into settlements that are too high. Again, the key is information and sharing that information to reach a fair and equitable settlement.

Fair & Equitable

The only way for a settlement negotiation to result in a fair and equitable indemnification is through complete and careful investigation, evaluation, and negotiation of all factors.

The only way for a settlement negotiation to result in a fair and equitable indemnification is through complete and careful investigation, evaluation, and negotiation of all factors. Unfortunately, many unsuccessful or imbalanced settlements begin with the adjuster negotiating damages. Damages should be the *last step* in a fair settlement negotiation, not the first.

The Ethical Negotiation Process

Coverage

The first area for investigation and evaluation is coverage. Many insureds have little understanding of their insurance coverage. They may be surprised to discover how comprehensive their first-part coverage actually is—or is not. Before a settlement can be accurate and fair, there must be mutual agreement on what the policy does and does not cover. For example, if the parties do not both understand a phrase such as actual cash value, how can they later agree on how much that value might be? Claimants often must be educated during this process, and the adjuster who provides the information must be knowledgeable about the subject.

Exclusions, limitations, and conditions that affect the claim must be explained to the insured. When coverage is questionable, a reservation of rights letter must be issued or nonwaiver agreement entered.

The coverage must be explained even in third-party claims in which there is no contractual agreement. However, the extent to which explanations are required for third-party claimants may differ legally from one jurisdiction to another. For example, most insurance claim experts believe that a third-party claimant has no right to know the maximum limit of coverage carried, unless the claim is so serious that it may be insufficient to settle the claim. In that case, disclosure and discussion with both the insured and the third party may be necessary.

In some jurisdictions evidence of insurance, and even the limits of liability, may be disclosed to adverse third parties. In California, for example, in some situations an uninsured motorist may not be entitled to collect general damages from an insured motorist, despite liability. In Florida, which is a direct action state, and perhaps in other states as well, a plaintiff is entitled to receive a copy of the insured's policy for confirmation of coverage and knowledge of the limits of liability.

Under the *Stowers* duty established in Texas, if a policy limit demand is made with a time limit for payment, and the payment is not made within that time limit—whether or not the third party knows the amount of the limits—the policy limits no longer apply. The insurer may be held liable for negligently failing to settle within the policy limits. In *Stowers,* the court held that an insurance company that controls the defense of a suit owes its insured a good faith duty to consider the interests of its clients as much as its own. Failure to exercise this care made the insurance company responsible for more than the policy limits. (See *Stowers Furniture Co. v. Am. Indemnity Co.,* 15 S.W.2d 544 [Tex. App. 1929]).

Coverage is the most significant factor in any settlement. Unless or until there is complete agreement between the parties on how the coverage applies, further negotiation toward settlement is probably unethical. It will lack the basic good faith requirement of understanding.

> **Coverage Is Critical**
>
> *Coverage is the most significant factor in any settlement. Unless or until there is complete agreement between the parties on how the coverage applies, further negotiation toward settlement is probably unethical. It will lack the basic good faith requirement of understanding.*

Liability

Investigation and evaluation of liability must be the next step. Too many claim representatives tend to relate liability solely to negligence issues. However, liability encompasses three areas of law: statutory, contract, and tort. Statutes can apply in many situations, from legislation involving employee injuries and no-fault laws to statutes of limitations, innkeeper statutes, and dog bite statutes. Jurisdictional statutes may affect settlement value.

Of the three areas, perhaps the most overlooked is that of contract law. Contractual agreements and limitations apply to almost any transaction between two parties. Typical contracts include premises leases, auto rental agreements, and equipment rental contracts. Contracts often may incorporate hold harmless agreements, waivers of subrogation, indemnity clauses, and insurance requirements—all of which can affect claims. Failure to honor a contractual agreement constitutes a breach of the contract. If claim representatives do not investigate and know about the contractual requirements, the contract may be breached. Failure to investigate and evaluate such conditions is extremely unethical.

Finally, all the rules regarding the law of tort must be considered. The rules differ among various jurisdictions with the laws where the loss occurred, rather than where the policy was issued, likely to control. Most states apply the rule of comparative negligence to negligence claims, but even these differ between modified and pure comparative negligence.

In a pure comparative negligence state, any degree of contributing negligence is offset against the other party, allowing recovery even if the injured party is 99 percent at fault and the insured only 1 percent at fault. In most modified comparative negligence states, an injured party cannot collect if he is more than 50 percent at fault in the accident. These rules are established either by state legislation or court interpretation. Since the rules differ among states, claim representatives must determine which rule applies and how it is interpreted in that jurisdiction. Failure to do so may result in an inequitable and unethical settlement.

Do You Agree?

When inadequate investigation results in an inability to negotiate liability factors, chances are that the resulting settlement will be inequitable.

When inadequate investigation results in an inability to negotiate liability factors, chances are that the resulting settlement will be inequitable: either overpaid or underpaid. If a claim file contains little more than an insured's accident report and a police report, there is a strong likelihood that significant liability factors may be overlooked.

Damages

The final element is that of damages. There are all sorts of damages: some are covered and some not, some are easily evaluated and others are not. Despite this variety in types of damages, they usually fall into three primary coverage areas: damage to or loss of tangible property, bodily or personal injury, and financial loss. The elements that are covered and to what extent are determined first by the insurance policy and then by the controlling liability.

For example, an automobile liability policy will cover property damage and bodily injury. It will not cover certain elements of personal injury, nor loss, which are strictly financial. If the insured slanders the claimant at the scene of an accident, or the claimant misses a vital appointment and loses out on a business deal worth thousands of dollars, the insured might be sued and found liable, but the policy will not cover the damages.

Damage to property is easier to evaluate than other types of damage. However, some property claims will become more difficult to evaluate in the twenty-first century as intangible property gains more importance through electronic business. Insurance professionals need to understand how both current and new forms of coverage address intangible property losses.

Valuation also is a typical area for property claim disputes. In actual cash value settlements, disputes often arise over how much depreciation should be charged against replacement cost. Identical items purchased by two different people may depreciate at different rates, depending on the care and use given the items. This can result in adjusters and claimants disagreeing on an equitable settlement value.

Even the use of replacement cost coverage has not totally eliminated valuation disputes. The insurer often retains the right to replace an item, which it usually can do for less than the insured might pay. In such a situation the parties must agree on what constitutes the settlement requirement for like kind and quality.

In the last half of the 1990s, disputes arose over the auto insurance industry's use of after-market or generic auto parts, which were cheaper than manufacturers' original equipment. The disputes led to litigation in a number of states, with some extremely high verdicts issued against insurers that had used such parts. Industry experts testified the parts were adequate, while other experts often termed the replacement parts substandard. (See summary, *CPCU Claims Quarterly*, Winter 2000 issue.)

Similar ethical issues arise in bodily injury claims. In this area there are *special damages*, which can be verified with a receipt or other document, and *general damages*, which are the intangible aspects of an injury. Even when medical costs are documented, other issues involving ethics may arise. One such issue is the *collateral source rule*, by which the victim receives compensation from other insurance sources that are not offset in a claim against the responsible tortfeasor.

Is it ethical for a claimant to collect payment for the same injuries from two sources?

Evaluation of general damages is even more difficult. How much is pain worth? How much is a crippling disability worth, beyond loss of earnings? Only by establishing a positive and active relationship with an injured person can insurance representatives build the trust and belief necessary to make such an evaluation.

Third-party claimants often retain attorneys to represent them. An insurer's representative may not ethically contact a represented claimant without her attorney's permission. So how can an understanding relationship be built? Certainly studying the documents surrounding the loss will help. Claim representatives who work in particular locations get to know the reputation of physicians and attorneys, which helps in the evaluation. Insurers usually are permitted legally to have injured claimants evaluated by a physician of their choice. Some physicians, however, may dedicate their practice to conducting independent medical examinations that habitually issue reports favorable to insurers and adverse to claimants. Far too often this results in protracted litigation.

> **Good Business?**
>
> *A fine line may exist between good business practices and those that involve questionable ethics.*

A fine line may exist between good business practices and those that involve questionable ethics. Many insurers in the 1990s and even earlier began to use paper reviews of claimants' medical records in place of actual physical examinations. Several outside firms offered this service to insurers on a fee basis, and it was demonstrated in one television news feature during 2000 that the reviews often were conducted by nonmedical personnel. It was alleged that many of the reports were drawn from standard computerized formats with little actual evaluation of the medical information provided. Is this type of system simply good business practice or an unethical way to save money?

But there is no law that prevents claim adjusters or attorneys from requesting a meeting with represented claimants. This may be helpful before an impasse results in litigation. Without an effort to investigate and evaluate, how can the right price for a claim be determined?

Ethics and Expectations: Understanding Emotions

Moral behavior and emotional behavior frequently are linked. If we see someone being injured or in need, the emotional response may be pity or sympathy, and the moral response may be to assist that person. If we observe a wrong being done, the emotional response may be anger, and the moral response may be to do something to correct the wrong. Therefore, emotions play a significant role in ethically responsible actions.

Importance of Emotions

The ability to recognize an emotional response becomes very important in the insurance setting, both in claim negotiation and marketing. Because emotions are so much a part of human behavior, we cannot understand another person until we understand his emotions.

The ability to recognize an emotional response becomes very important in the insurance setting, both in claim negotiation and marketing. Because emotions are so much a part of human behavior, we cannot understand another person until we understand his emotions. This is often referred to as empathy, something quite different from sympathy.

Making an effort to understand a customer's emotional, as well as physical, needs can open doors to a long-lasting business relationship. For example, a customer may express anger because of an insurance-related incident: a cancellation, a rate increase, or the need to go into an assigned risk pool. It may be simple to figure out why the customer is angry, but merely filling the customer's need does not resolve the underlying problem. Understanding the emotions requires getting to the root of their cause.

Why was there a cancellation? If it was the customer's own fault, helping him determine that and then working with him to avoid future similar problems will go a lot further than simply avoiding discussion. If the problem lies with the insurer—a rate increase or a decision not to underwrite in a certain state—determining the reason and developing a solution may result in a lasting relationship.

If the problem is one of insurer unfairness, the agent or broker may have to help to resolve the problem directly or assist the customer complain to state insurance regulators.

Recognizing the emotional resentment that many customers feel toward the insurance industry may lead to a better business relationship, morally and ethically superior to any prior relationship. An agent or broker may turn a negative situation into a positive, active response, one that even might produce additional business. Is this ethical? Of course it is!

A life insurance agent recounts that an acquaintance applied for coverage and was sent to a physician for a physical examination. The exam uncovered a serious, but curable, health condition. The insurer declined to write the policy, and the customer underwent expensive treatment. The customer was angry until the agent explained, "It saved your life!" The customer then saw the matter in a different light. After he was cured, the coverage was re-underwritten and a policy was issued.

Understanding emotions is especially important in the claim arena. With the exception of the simple claims, it is vitally important for adjusters or attorneys to meet with the parties involved. Emotions can be detected in many ways. Voices can reveal resignation, anger, fear, hostility, or sorrow. Body language often indicates emotions, as do facial expressions and eye contact. These cannot be observed over the telephone. While loss and claims are everyday events for the claim representative, they usually are unique experiences for the claimant or insured, who may fear or resent the claims process. After all, that process invades individuals' privacy and upsets life's normal routines.

> **Disclosure Is Key**
>
> *Claim explanations and discussions must be open and complete because the key to fair dealing is disclosure.*

Claim explanations and discussions must be truthful, accurate, and firm. But more importantly they must be open and complete because the key to fair dealing is disclosure. Neither should they act in an intimidating manner. Despite the award-winning Robert Ringer book of two decades ago, *Winning Through Intimidation*, intimidating actions will result only in trouble for the claims process.

Moral Responses and Ethical Solutions

As discussed in the fourth edition of *Casualty Insurance Claims* (Magarick and Brownlee, 1995), it is likely that hostility toward the party for the damages may be transferred toward the claim representative. When this happens, what is the moral response, the ethical solution? How much responsibility should the claim representative take for the situation? Certainly that will be limited by the coverage available. Very little coverage may result in very little response. Very high limits, however, may deeply involve the representative in everything from rehabilitation to structured settlements. But can the insurer ethically abandon an insured once limits are exhausted? Is there an obligation to assist an insured determine whether the adverse party had other resources, whether the law might provide an alternative remedy, or whether various public agencies might be able to assist the insured? These are the real moral and ethical issues for consideration.

Many insurance claim specialists might argue that there is no such obligation, that the duty of the insurer is limited to settlement and defense within the terms of the contract. There is considerable argument that subrogation—the process of trying to recoup any payments made from the tortfeasor—is legally limited to what the insurer has paid, plus perhaps the insured's deductibles. Many experts suggest that subrogation is a waste of time and energy anyway, for it amounts only to swapping money back and forth between insurers. Actions beyond simply recovering claim payments would be extra-contractual, leading to the insurer practicing law.

In spite of these possibilities, can there be an ethical obligation to explore possible avenues of recovery and to disclose that information to the insured?

Blowing the Whistle: Is It Fraud, Greed, Anger, Exaggeration, or Error?

Because each situation creates its own ethical dilemmas, decision-making is largely predicated upon individual experiences, attitudes, and political and social philosophy, as well as the influence of family, friends, the media, religion, and other institutions. There are at least two viewpoints on practically any issue.

One common issue that may affect an organization's ethical stance is its response to a whistle-blower, someone who publicly reveals proprietary information that leads to civil litigation or criminal indictments. While the law may protect—even award—whistle blowers from retaliation, the typical reaction among their peers is shock and shunning. After all, such actions often jeopardize everyone's employment, regardless of involvement in the wrongful action or not. Whistleblowers can be heroes, but few are treated as such. And sometimes they are mistaken; their facts are in error. What should the moral and ethical response be to whistle blowing?

Changed Attitudes?

Since insurance fraud has been placed in the spotlight, attitudes toward those making claims have changed.

Most people as children have been on both sides of the issue, at times tattling on others and at others being tattled on. That is normal. However, when behaviors get out of balance, unethical results can occur.

This can be seen in the area of insurance claims. Since insurance fraud has been placed in the spotlight, attitudes toward those making claims have changed. Claim representatives are carefully trained to watch for fraud indicators, a list of behaviors that individually may mean nothing but in combination suggest potential fraud. High on the list is a desire for a quick settlement, which, ironically, is the public's number one demand from the insurance industry.

However, when adjusters can demonstrate that there was no loss and the claim is fraudulent, there is a crime, and it must be reported. In most cases this results in a simple denial of the claim and cancellation of coverage.

Insurer claim representatives and special investigation units occasionally go beyond simple denial and bring legal action against those they believe have perpetrated the fraud. Such cases, including reverse bad faith claims, rarely are successful in court. Legal action instigated by an insurer often opens the door to counteractions, including allegations of slander, libel, defamation of character, malicious prosecution, or false arrest. If the insurer's evidence of fraud is insufficient to prove criminal intent and the accused is exonerated, the insurer probably will lose the personal injury counter claim.

In some states, insurers are not even permitted to claim restitution for claims they have paid and for which the insured gets restitution from the party causing the damage. For example, in *People v. Birkett*, 980 P. 2d 912 (1999), the California Supreme Court ruled that an insurer is not entitled to receive restitution for crime-related losses of its insured that had been paid by the insurer. The *Birkett* case involved a chop shop that stole insured vehicles and stripped them for resale of the parts. The court found that the "direct victim" was the insured, not the insurance company that paid the claims. Since the law provided for restitution of only the "direct victim," insurers were not entitled to recovery.

However, in the subsequent California case of *People v. Moloy,* 84 Cal. App. 4th 257 (2000), the appellate court upheld an insurer's right of recovery because it was the direct victim of the fraud. The *Moloy* case involved an elaborate scheme of staged accidents with physicians and attorneys participating. Insurance companies were the object of the *Moloy* scheme so could obtain restitution.

The insurance company, known as the surety, does have a right of recovery in various types of bonds, including fiduciary and fidelity bonds. The difficulty with fidelity (employee dishonesty) bond claims is that the employer (the obligee) has the responsibility of determining the amount of loss and of indicating the suspect employee(s), although there is no requirement that they be identified, arrested or prosecuted. The employer must file a proof of loss, and the surety investigates that document—not the alleged crime. The surety thus may be insulated from potential personal injury allegations that might arise from a disagreement between the accused employee and the employer as to the crime or the amount of the loss.

What is the moral and ethical response to such difficult scenarios? It definitely is not to become naïve about fraud, nor to look the other way. There must be ethically responsible action.

Information, Imagination, Ingenuity

The ethically responsible action involves key requirements of information, imagination, and ingenuity. Adjusters must, to some degree, view the facts from the claimant's viewpoint. Obviously, if the claim is totally criminal, that must be documented, the claim denied, and the matter referred to the proper authorities. But if a real loss seems suspicious, the situation must be carefully investigated and analyzed.

When doing so, we must remember that greed is not a crime. If a preposterously high demand is made, an adjuster might ask why the claimant believes that would be fair and equitable compensation. He might explain that the state Unfair Claims Practices Act requires the insurer to settle claims fairly and equitably. If the person mentions a friend who got that much or a recently publicized high verdict, the adjuster may be able to explain the differences between the cases.

Another common reaction is to exaggerate damages. Adjusters know the typical ones: "The car will *never* be the same after that wreck!" "I'll probably *always* have this pain!" "I've *never* had so much agony!" Sometimes these statements may be true; often they are simply reactions, emotional responses that reflect anger, bitterness, hostility, and revenge. Such emotions also are not crimes!

Occasionally, a claim representative encounters the opposite type, a person who seems barely interested in being compensated for loss. The adjuster may be tempted in such cases to take advantage of the person. However, he must clearly understand attitudes and emotions in these circumstances as well. Why would a person feel remorse and reject indemnification? In cases of comparative negligence, the response may be one of guilt. Perhaps there is a feeling that the insurance settlement is charity or welfare. (It is not!) Many people do not like to discuss negative aspects of their lives with others and may rationalize difficulties. Claim representatives who try to understand these motivations are likely to establish a positive relationship that will lead to a good faith settlement.

> **Understanding Relationships**
>
> *Insurance ethics are largely wrapped up in creating understanding relationships based on accurate information and positive action. That is both the moral and the legal basis upon which insurance must stand.*

Insurance ethics are largely wrapped up in creating understanding relationships based on accurate information and positive action. That is both the moral and the legal basis upon which insurance must stand.

Thought Provokers

1. An agent is concerned about a young customer who has accumulated several traffic tickets and just purchased a sports car. Is simply placing the young man in the assigned risk pool and collecting the premium an ethical solution? Does it result in positive action? Should the agent do anything else?

2. Consider what would be an ethical response to the following situation. A woman has fallen on some debris in a grocery store and is claiming that her right hip and shoulder are injured. The woman tells the claim adjuster that she has had no prior injuries. An Index Bureau review shows that the woman fell in a store several years earlier and injured her right side. What should the adjuster do?

3. What ethical action could be taken in the following situation? Auditors for a small casualty insurance company discover that claim data had been recorded in a way that nearly doubled claim costs. The vice president of claims already was terminated for failing to control claim costs, and the insurer filed for a rate increase before the problem was discovered. What should the insurer do?

Chapter 6

More than Avoiding a Conflict of Interest

"Ethics implies 'conflicts in morality'."

Aristotle

E thics is much more than mere moralizing over what to do or not to do—it must encompass a deep moral philosophy based on virtue, moral worth, character, responsibility, and excellence in disposition. It must be much more than simply codes of ethics or a system of rules and laws.

In the field of law, the most feared ethical breach often is considered to be any form of a conflict of interest. Such a conflict for an attorney can arise in many forms: representing one client in a matter involving another client, commingling of client funds with firm funds, accepting favors from someone to influence how one deals with a client, too close a relationship with a judge or jury member.

Conflict of interest can arise in any field. We occasionally hear of physicians or scientists who have made self-serving statements or pushed medications or products in which they have a financial interest—perhaps not illegal, but at a minimum ethically questionable.

In the field of insurance, conflict of interest also can be a major ethical problem, although much of it is hidden in the mechanisms of the business. An agent or broker has a conflict of interest to some extent whenever that person tries to sell a customer more or the wrong kind of insurance simply because of a higher commission.

Hidden Problem?

In the field of insurance, conflict of interest also can be a major ethical problem, although much of it is hidden in the mechanisms of the business.

When a company tightens its claim processes to the point where they border on unfairness simply to improve the bottom line, there is a conflict of interest. For claim representatives, individual conflicts of interest arise on almost a daily basis.

There often is a temptation to help someone we personally like—an insured or claimant—and to stiff someone we do not like. It might, therefore, be a conflict of interest for an adjuster to handle the claim of a personal friend or relative. There is a conflict for an adjuster to direct repair work to a business in which she has a financial stake or from which she receives commission or compensation. It is a conflict for a claims representative to receive a fee from a law firm for referring clients. Conflicts of interest often arise simply in the way business is conducted—the amount of time spent on a particular situation. Time, as well as money, can create conflicts. Most of us have more to do than time to do it. The kinds of decisions made on how to use available time can determine whether we avoid conflicts or rush and do not act professionally.

Time and Money

Time, as well as money, can create conflicts. Most of us have more to do than time to do it. The kinds of decisions made on how to use available time can determine whether we avoid conflicts or rush and do not act professionally.

According to Bertrand Russell in *A History of Western Philosophy,* Aristotle suggested that there are "two kinds of virtues, *intellectual* and *moral,* corresponding to the two parts of the soul. Intellectual virtues result from teaching, moral virtues from habit. It is the business of the legislator to make the citizens good by forming good habits. We become just by performing just acts, and similarly as regards other virtues. By being compelled to acquire good habits, we shall in time, Aristotle thinks, come to find pleasure in performing good actions."

Russell explains that Aristotle's concept of moral issues was conventional for his day but does differ on some points. According to Russell, "We think that human beings, at least in ethical theory, all have equal rights, and that justice involves equality; Aristotle thinks that justice involves, not equality, but right proportion, which is only *sometimes* equality." Perhaps it is this that creates the conflicts in what we consider to be moral.

Claim Adjustment Versus Loss Adjustment

There is a difference between a *loss* and a *claim.* Loss is a dynamic process, some combination of factors—hazards—that build into an accident or is named as a specific peril. But the event itself is not the end of loss. Taking on a life of its own, loss continues to spread direct and indirect damage. A claim, on the other hand, is simply a financial transaction, often under a contract such as an insurance policy or governed by some aspect of law. Some define a claim as a *demand*.

Whether the factors that lead to loss are natural or man-made, it is possible to intervene at various points to either prevent the loss or diminish the amount of damage. This is why the fields of risk management, claim adjusting, and insurance are so closely related.

The loss control side of risk management, which includes identifying and treating hazards and implementing methods to deal with those hazards, applies to both preloss and postloss action. Neither fire extinguishers nor sprinkler systems can prevent a fire from starting; these are postloss control devices to decrease damage. An auto air bag does not prevent auto collisions; it is designed to reduce injuries. A guardrail along a dangerous highway, however, actually may prevent a vehicle from going over the side of the road.

Loss adjusting must take all of these factors into consideration. It must be concerned with what happened and why it happened, not just with the cost of resulting damage. The information that is obtained may help to prevent similar losses, to reduce the continuing direct or indirect loss, or to recoup some of the financial damages. In property losses, for example, postloss control includes using salvage operations to recoup some financial loss or expediting repairs to reduce indirect loss. In injury claims, postloss control includes medical cost-containment procedures such as utilization review and rehabilitation to restore an injured person to a useful occupation. In both types of loss, subrogation against responsible tortfeasors is a postloss control procedure.

Too often, unfortunately, the insurance industry is interested only in completing the claims aspect of loss. It is relatively easy to calculate the bare minimum degree of service and financial payment due and to make that the maximum of commitment. That is perfectly legal— it is exactly what the contract provides—but it often fails to comply with the broader roles of insurance: to produce useful information, to provide peace of mind, or even to fully indemnify. The difference between *adjusting the claim* and *adjusting the loss* often is one of ethical consideration.

The Ethics of Adjusting the Loss

Pareto's Law (the 80/20 Rule) provides that in any large number of factors—any kind of factors—a small percentage will consume the largest percentage of time, action, or money. This is especially true in risk management. A handful of situations consume most of the time of those involved.

This is significant in claim adjusting. Thousands of small claims can be resolved with little or no effort, especially when using computer data banks and other electronic communication methods. A handful of major losses, however, will not resolve easily and demand the time and attention—and personal hands-on activity that a computer cannot provide. Size of the loss is not necessarily the determining factor. Many large, expensive claims resolve quickly and simply, while smaller ones may take months or years to resolve.

Small matters should be handled quickly. The fender-bender auto claim, the minor injury doctor's bill, the stolen bicycle—all of these require little outside action or hand holding with those involved. They undoubtedly make up the bulk of claims, easily handled by phone, mail, and computer. Such is not the case for a larger, serious loss.

> **Time and Attention**
>
> *Size of the loss is not necessarily the determining factor. Many large, expensive claims resolve quickly and simply, while smaller ones may take months or years to resolve.*

In any type of loss where there is extensive damage, serious injury, death, or indirect loss factors, the *loss* as well as the *claim* must be adjusted. All the facts of the loss must be obtained to determine exactly what caused it—and to ferret out possible sources of subrogation. This process helps the claim representative get to know and understand the injured party and begin to build a positive relationship that will lead to a good faith settlement.

The claim representative is not in charge; that duty always must fall to the individual who has suffered the loss. The insurer's representative cannot direct the recovery, select the physician or repair facility, and demand that only those she selected be used. However, she must be in control. That is why it is necessary to establish a positive understanding relationship when adjusting the loss.

When a loss disrupts the lifestyle of the victim or the business of an enterprise, the loss adjuster must become involved in order to control the loss. Often the victims do not know what to do. Loss is usually a new experience for them. Monetary indemnity, while necessary, often is not their primary concern.

This is where adjusting the loss as opposed to simply adjusting the claim becomes significant. An insurance policy does not require the insurer to explain the process (although many state unfair claim practices acts do). It does not require the insurer's representative to hold the victim's hand or express concern, to offer suggestions, or to bring order out of the chaos that is the loss. The law does not mandate that an insurer's representatives use every available loss-settlement technique to help resolve the trauma of the loss. The law even requires that the person making the claim prove the claim. But remember: the law is the minimum standard of behavior; ethics is the highest.

This is not a how-to text, but there is a system by which one can quickly learn how to adjust the loss ethically. Some of the salient points of that system are:

1. Upon assignment, immediately contact the claim-ant. In serious losses, persist until actual contact is made.

2. Explain the official role and standing of the adjuster with reference to the insurance policy or the law. Begin to establish a relationship with the claimant.

3. Take the first steps to establish such a relation-ship when obtaining information. That information falls into three areas: coverage, liability, and damages. The adjuster also has a duty to pre-serve the evidence, which may be written or oral statements, physical or tangible evidence, pho-tographs, or documents such as bills and re-ceipts.

4. Be empathetic. The adjuster's attitude often will help to control the loss victim's response.

5. Stress the importance of accurate information. Without accurate information, evaluation and settlement will be difficult and, likely, inequitable.

6. Explain what the adjuster, under the policy or the law, can and cannot do. After obtaining necessary and accurate information, summarize the situation for the claimant and explain the plan for recovery.

7. Try to mentally step into the shoes of the victim. This requires imagination. Imagine the loss as it occurred and as it is continuing to develop in order to assist in controlling it.

One of the most difficult aspects of loss adjusting is when the process breaks down and the understanding relationship between the loss victim and the adjuster becomes hostile. This is not necessarily the fault of the adjuster. People who have suffered a loss have a variety of emotions and motivations. The hostility toward a tortfeasor who caused the damage may be transferred to the claim representative.

The Ethics of Adjusting the Claim

A claim is simply a financial transaction. It is created at the time and place of occurrence. The laws of the jurisdiction in which the loss occurred control the claim. Those laws differ, and the adjuster must understand those differences if the claim is to be adjusted correctly.

An adjuster may be assigned a third-party claim that arises from an auto accident that occurred in a different state. That state's contributory or comparative negligence laws can control whether any claim—or the amount of the claim—is owed. The adjuster also must consider statutes of limitations or unique aspects of local laws that may differ from those in the jurisdiction where the claim is being settled.

For example, consider a claimant from Detroit who was involved in an accident in Tennessee when she was driving to Florida. The insurer for the responsible Tennessee insured hired a Florida adjuster to handle the claim while the claimant was staying in Florida. The damage to her automobile was repaired and paid for by the Tennessee insurer. The claimant was still being treated for her injuries when she decided to return to Detroit, and the Florida adjuster transferred the claim to a Michigan adjuster.

When time came for her to return to Florida, the claimant decided to confer with the physician in Florida who had done the initial treatment. She therefore asked the Michigan adjuster to again transfer the file back to the Florida adjuster. The woman returned to her Florida home for the winter.

A month or so later she was discharged by the Florida physician, and the adjuster agreed to contact the Tennessee insurer for authority for final settlement. However, the Tennessee insurance company advised him to close the file. Tennessee has a one-year bodily injury statute of limitations, and it had expired. Upon being informed of this, the claimant hired a Florida attorney and sued the adjuster.

> **Who Ends Up Paying?**
>
> *The adjusters had done a fairly good job of adjusting the loss, but they had failed to adjust the claim. The financial transaction, or claim payment, became the responsibility of the independent adjuster because he failed to consider laws of the jurisdiction in which the loss occurred.*

In this case the adjusters had done a fairly good job of adjusting the loss, but they had failed to adjust the claim. The financial transaction, or claim payment, became the responsibility of the independent adjuster because he failed to consider laws of the jurisdiction in which the loss occurred.

Understanding the Adjustment Process

Exactly what does the term *adjustment* mean in reference to a loss and the resulting claim? Every claim representative in the country might have his own definition, which might include reference to resolving a claim with either payment or denial. The word *compromise* might play a role. Some might define adjustment in terms of protecting the insurer and the insured from unjust demands. Others might refer to terminology such as that in the NAIC Model Unfair Claims Settlement Practice Act, to "settle claims in good faith fairly, promptly and equitably whenever liability is reasonably clear." However, many of these terms are vague and unclear. Fair, prompt, and equitable compromises are difficult to define.

By beginning any adjustment with careful analysis of the coverage, an adjuster can move quickly to establish the understanding relationship so necessary for a good faith resolution of the claim. When coverage does not apply to all or part of the loss, the parties must be informed and agree on that fact so the claim can be resolved, even if that means a denial of the claim. In the Mississippi case of *Sobley v. Southern Natural Gas Co.*, 210 F.3d 561 (5th U.S. Cir. 2000), the court found that a reasonable basis for denying a claim will not defeat a bad faith allegation if the insurer fails to identify the coverage issue to the insured before denying coverage.

Liability is significant, but a liability investigation must be secondary to that of coverage. In *Fulton* (See *Lloyd's & Inst. of London Underwriting v. Fulton*, 2 P.3 1199 [Ak. 2000]), the insurer's failure to notify its insured of potential coverage defenses before taking statements from the insured estopped the insurer from using those defenses. If there is no coverage, liability and damages are moot points. If coverage is doubtful, the adjuster may explore liability under a reservation of rights or a nonwaiver agreement as part of the loss adjustment. This opens up opportunities for an insured or third party to explore on his or her own.

Finally, all aspects of damages must be examined. Coverage may apply to only direct, or only indirect, or perhaps both types of damage. It may apply only to damage from certain perils. All this must be evaluated and negotiated—agreed upon.

Avoiding Bad Faith Claims

Most bad faith claims arise out of third-party claims against an insured in which the insurer fails to act in the best interests of its insured. There are, however, a number of ways in which an insurer can be found to have acted in bad faith against the insured in a first-party claim. Courts differ as to what this means and on whether there must be a specific contractual duty for there to be a breach of that duty. The usual situation involves an allegation that settlement of a claim was denied or delayed by the insurer deliberately, when the insurer "knew or should have known" that the delay or denial was damaging the insured and was unfounded.

Each month cases involving allegations of bad faith are reported. These cases usually come to public attention when they involve large punitive damages awards.

Bad Faith and Publicity

Cases alleging bad faith usually come to public attention when they involve large punitive damages awards.

In the first-party bad faith claim of *Zilisch v. State Farm,* 995 P.2d 276 (Az. 2000) the Arizona Supreme Court ruled that bad faith issues of whether an insurer acted unreasonably in investigating, evaluating, and processing a claim and either knew or consciously disregarded the fact that its conduct was unreasonable are issues of fact for jury decision. That the value of the claim was debatable did not necessarily entitle the insurer to a directed verdict.

Many first-party claims involve health insurance. It may be difficult for an insured to bring a claim, for health-insurance programs that are provided as employee benefits are subject to ERISA. Therefore, they are a matter for federal rather than state courts. Despite some inroads of state jurisdiction over health-insurance matters, the federal government probably will maintain jurisdiction for the foreseeable future.

In the New Jersey case of *In re: U.S. Healthcare, Inc.,* 193 F.3d 151 (3rd U.S. Cir. 1999), however, the federal court ruled that ERISA's civil enforcement provision did not preempt claims against the plaintiff's health maintenance organization. The lawsuit alleged that the HMO's policy of discharging infants from a hospital within twenty-four hours after birth had been a direct cause of the infant's later death. Likewise, in a Wisconsin case, the state's supreme court allowed a bad faith claim against an HMO that alleged unreasonable refusal to authorize an out-of-network referral. (See *McEvoy v. Group Health Cooperative,* 570 N.W.2d 397 [1997].)

Another aspect of first-party bad faith claims involves the burden of proof. Many denials of coverage or delays in settlement arise when a fraudulent claim is suspected. Although an insurer must be able to prove criminal intent beyond the shadow of a reasonable doubt to win in criminal court, it can demonstrate fraud in a civil court with only a preponderance of the evidence. This rule, however, becomes a double-edged sword. If the insurer is unable to prove the insured's fraud with a preponderance of the evidence, it may have acted in bad faith. Its failure to prove fraud becomes evidence for the insured, who also may prove bad faith with the same degree of preponderance of the evidence.

In the Texas case of *Simmons,* (*State Farm Fire & Cas. Co. v. Simmons,* 963 S.W.2d 42 [1998]), that state's supreme court found that there was sufficient evidence to support the jury's bad faith verdict (but not its punitive damage award) against the insurer for having conducted a "biased" investigation intended to prove, unsuccessfully, that the insured had committed arson. A California court, however, ruled in *Roberts v. Sentry Life Ins. Co.,* 90 Cal.Rptr.2d 408 (2nd Dist, Div. 7, 1999) that an insurer suing an insured for fraud could not be held liable for malicious prosecution unless the insured was entitled to summary judgment on the insurer's fraud allegations.

In third-party actions, however, it is not the third party that usually brings the bad faith action against the insurer, except in cases in which an insured transfers that right to the third party, a procedure that is permitted in several states. In North Carolina, for instance, such an assignment was prohibited by the appellate court in *Terrell v. Lawyers Mutl. Ins. Co of N.C.,* 507 S.E.2d 923 (1998). Most states do not recognize a duty of good faith to a third party. That duty arises solely out of the contractual agreements between the insured and the insurance company. An Illinois court ruled, for example, that an insurer had a duty to act in good faith in settling a claim against an insured both before and after a lawsuit is filed. (See *Haddick v. Valor Ins.,* 735 N.E.2d 132 [Ill. 3rd Dist. 2000].)

Other bad faith claims have arisen out of an insurer's attempt to make its settlement conditional on some factor, and an adverse result subsequently occurred. The Montana Supreme Court, for example, has prohibited a liability insurer from using the settlement condition of release of its insured for payment of the policy limits, when the limits are clearly owed. (*Watters v. Guaranty Natl. Ins. Co.,* 3 P.2d 626 [2000]). Massachusetts also had a similar ruling in *Kapp v. Arbella Mutl. Ins. Co.,* 689 N.E.2d 1347 (1998). However, not all states agree on this point. To illustrate, in Texas, under *Trinity Universal Ins. Co. v. Bleeker,* 966 S.W.2d 489 (Tx. App. 1998), an insurer is not obligated to accept settlement offers that do not fully release the insured from liability. In one California case, the insurer's offer to pay its policy limits in a claim against the insured was found to be in bad faith where it was conditioned on the insured abandoning rights on a first-party coverage. (See *Shade Foods, Inc. v. Innovative Products,* 93 Cal.Rptr.2d 364 [App. 1st Dist., 2000].)

Other Problems for Insurers

Bad faith actions often result from serious claims in which the insured has only limited coverage. For example, an insured has an auto liability policy that provides a combined single limit of $100,000. The insured negligently hits and seriously injures two pedestrians: a sixty-eight-year-old married woman and a thirty-five-year-old father of three. The man suffers permanent injuries that leave him unable to work for many years and also incurs more than $130,000 in medical bills. Two days later the woman dies. The amount of coverage will not in any way indemnify the victims of this accident. How the insurer proceeds will determine whether it can correctly—and ethically— settle the claim for the $100,000 worth of coverage.

This issue of too many claims and not enough money was explored by a Georgia court in *Miller v. Ga. Interlocal Risk Mgt. Agency,* 501 S.E.2d 589 (1998), with the appellate court ruling that settlement of one claim that used most of the combined single policy limit, leaving the other claim unsettled, was not bad faith. That state's case law demonstrates the position that a liability insurer does not have a duty to consider the interests of third-party claimants when deciding how to distribute policy limits that are inadequate to compensate all the claimants. When the limits are split, settlement for less than the occurrence limit by paying the per person limit also may not be bad faith. In *Redcross v. Aetna C&S Co.,* 688 N.Y.S.2d 817 (N.Y. App. 1999) the insured had $100/300 thousand limits; there were several claimants who proposed a package deal that would have exceeded the per person limits but did not exceed the per occurrence limit. The insurer's refusal to accept the package demand was determined not to be in bad faith.

Good Faith Lies in Good Communication

What should the insurer ethically do when a claim or lawsuit may result in an award in excess of policy limits? First, it must act quickly to advise the insured that the claim probably will exceed the policy limits. This is done through an *excess letter.* If there are other coverage problems, the insured must be advised, usually through a reservation of rights letter. Coverage issues should be resolved as quickly as possible. Again, the key to good faith lies in good communication. The insured and the insurer should be partners. For example, a New York court in *Smith v. General Accident Ins. Co.,* 674 N.Y.S.2d 267 (1998) ruled that an insurer's failure to keep its insured informed of settlement negotiations was evidence of bad faith.

The insured and insurer should anticipate that there will be litigation if the matter is not resolved. Therefore early and positive contact with the claimant or his legal representative is mandatory. Many insurers are reluctant to reveal policy limits. A potential excess situation—absent umbrella or other excess liability coverages—may not be such a case. The insurer must be candid with the claimant or attorney, advising of the limited coverage available and offering it as soon as possible in exchange for a release of further claims against the insured. Even when excess coverage is available, the insurer may owe a good faith duty to that excess carrier to settle within the primary policy limits if possible. Any excess insurer is also a partner.

How might the insurer accidentally step into the pit of bad faith in this difficult situation? Various courts have found there to be bad faith from any of the following actions:

1. Attempting to argue comparative negligence as a means of saving on the policy limits where the third party's negligence, if any, is either remote or so slight as to have no effect on the difference between the value of the *loss* (the total of damages) and the amount of coverage.

2. Attempting to get the insured to add something to the settlement pot in order to gain a release.

3. Offering the policy limits without any attempt to obtain a release of the insured for the amount paid. One version of this, accepted by some courts but not by others, is payment of policy limits to the court for distribution in exchange for the court's release of the insurer from the obligations of the policy.

4. Failing to attempt to settle the case before litigation is filed. Once litigation is filed, the insurer is obliged to defend the insured and to keep the insured informed on the status of the litigation and settlement negotiations.

5. In some states, the court may invalidate policy limits if an insurer fails to respond to a demand for payment of the policy limits. (See *Stowers Furniture Co v. Am. Indem. Co.,* 15 S.W.2d 544 [Texas 1929].)

6. Failing to defend the insured properly or forcing the insured to retain his or her own counsel to defend prior to exhaustion of policy limits.

7. Failing to thoroughly investigate, which results in an adverse effect.

While bad faith claims receive a tremendous amount of publicity, they actually are rare and usually result from very outrageous and deceptive actions by the insurer.

Typical Insurer Codes of Ethics: "Thou Shalt Not..."

Consultants in business ethics frequently recommend a process for instilling a sense of ethical behavior into an organization. It often follows a four-step plan that includes writing a code of ethics, establishing an ethics committee, hiring a person to train executives and employees in ethics, and communicating the need for ethics to all employees. Compliance with such a plan undoubtedly will be a major step toward ethical practices by the firm.

Unfortunately, many organizations get no further than the first step, writing a code

> **Four-step Process**
>
> *Instilling a sense of ethical behavior into an organization often follows a four-step plan that includes writing a code of ethics, establishing an ethics committee, hiring a person to train executives and employees in ethics, and communicating the need for ethics to all employees.*

of ethics. Too often such codes are little more than rulebooks or a list of dos and don'ts.

One organization that follows through on the four-step plan is the CPCU Society, which not only has a Code of Ethics but a standing ethics committee, regular publication of ethics material, and ethics training within the curriculum for students seeking to become Chartered Property & Casualty Underwriters. The code, however, is simple, and not strewn with rules: "As a Chartered Property and Casualty Under-writer I shall strive at all times to live by the highest standards of professional conduct; I shall strive to ascertain and understand the needs of others and place their interests above my own; and I shall strive to maintain and uphold a standard of honor and integrity that will reflect credit upon my profession and on the CPCU designation."

Ten Rules for Adjusters

Some rules of ethics for adjusters include:

1. Adjusters may not accept gifts or payments from parties with whom they are doing business.

2. Adjusters and appraisers may not deal in the salvage of property in the claims they handle nor make referrals to businesses in which they have a financial interest.

3. Charges and expenses incurred must be accurately recorded and verified in the billing process.

4. An adjuster cannot represent both sides in a claim or handle a claim that involves a friend, relative, or someone with whom the adjuster has a financial relationship.

5. The adjuster must not deal directly with an insured or third party that is represented by counsel with-out that attorney's direct permission.

6. The adjuster must clearly identify herself—and disclose all parties the adjuster represents—to any

person she contacts. Any person from whom a taped statement is obtained should acknowledge that they are being recorded.

7. The adjuster must protect the interests of any party with a financial interest in the claim and of those covered by the policy.

8. In evaluating damages, the adjuster must take into account all applicable aspects of the damage, such as proper depreciation, correct pricing and calculations, and the value of intangible aspects of the loss.

9. An adjuster or appraiser should not copy the estimate of any repair facility or contractor and present it as his own.

10. The adjuster should not act as a witness to any document he has drawn or completed, such as a release or sworn statement in proof of loss.

Typical of such rules is the code of ethics of the National Association Independent Insurance Adjusters, as published in the *NAIIA Blue Book*. This code includes not only rules but also truly ethical practices and procedures.

While many codes of ethics used in the insurance industry refer to professionalism, few include any reference to continuing education or an educational standard for the profession, which is unfortunate. Professional ethics must include both educational aspects and altruism.

> **Two Aspects**
>
> *Professional ethics must include both educational aspects and altruism.*

Responsibility: Taking Control, Not Taking Charge

This ethical principle was discussed in some detail in Chapter 2. It is an important rule in handling claims, for there always is the temptation for both the damaged party and the adjuster to allow the adjuster to take over completely, regardless of the situation. While the adjuster must be in control, that control should be leveraged through the parties who have suffered the loss.

The degree to which an insurer can control defense litigation has come into considerable dispute in recent years because of two factors primarily focused on cost containment. First is the increased use of house counsel (attorneys directly employed by the insurer to defend insureds) and the use of captive firms, those which are owned wholly or in part by the insurer or in which the insurer has some controlling interest, and, second, is attorney fee auditing. Legal fee auditing involves referring legal bills to outside legal bill auditing firms that review, and often revise, charges that do not comply with the insurer's published litigation instructions. Several courts have ruled that billing audits cannot be conducted unless the insured agrees, since the bill—and any file material provided by the insurer to the auditor for verification—technically are confidential client information of the insured.

Whether these legal cost containment procedures are ethical or not could be debated, but, except in cases in which the insured withholds authorization for bill auditing, the procedures are legal. Litigation management—but not supervisory direction of defense counsel—is necessary in the claim adjustment process. On the other hand, if the direction of the litigation becomes either punitive or the cost-cutting so severe that outside defense attorney can no longer devote the time and attention necessary to properly handle the lawsuit, an adverse effect occurs that benefits neither the insured nor the insurer. The ethics in this debate call for an equitable balance between the need for litigation management and the need for defense independence.

Claims Don't Come With Bar Codes

It is important to keep in mind that neither the losses that give rise to claims nor the thousand variables among coverage, liability, and damage issues of those resulting claims are standard. To individuals involved in the *loss*, each *claim* is unique. When those investigating and evaluating the claims rely too heavily on standardized information, there can be negative and unethical results.

Each Claim Is Unique

To individuals involved in the loss, each claim is unique. When those investigating and evaluating the claims rely too heavily on standardized information, there can be negative and unethical results.

The use of data banks and Internet resources has greatly enhanced the ability of claim adjusters and attorneys to obtain necessary data. Information such as driving records, weather, highway directions, medical conditions, and pricing can be obtained at the click of a mouse. But the claim representative has a duty to verify the accuracy of such information, especially as it applies to the individual claim.

For example, an insurance company's computer system may show an insured's coverage, exclusions, conditions, and endorsements. But reviewing this information is only a part of the coverage investigation. The circumstances of the claim also must be examined to see if they fit the scope of coverage. Recent changes that may impact the claim may not have made their way to the computer.

To illustrate, suppose an insured gives his new wife, who has a sixteen-year-old son, a car. The insured notifies the agent of these changes. However, if an accident involving the new car and the sixteen-year-old occurs before the insurer has updated the data in its computer system, the claim may be denied. Rejecting the claim solely because of the computer data would not only lead to unnecessary litigation, it would be unethical. Such a claim should be investigated.

One aspect of claim evaluation is setting reserves. Insurers use a variety of methods, ranging from case reserves to block reserves for particular types of claims. It usually falls to the individual claim representative to set the individual file reserve. Some may do so solely on the basis of experience, without regularly adjusting the reserve as the investigation continues. The result is that the reserve may be too high or too low. Either way, the reserve fails to meet even the business ethic of buying and selling at the proper price, and the practice of improperly reserving the claim becomes an act of professional misfeasance.

Many claim evaluation services are available *online*, advising what juries have awarded in similar cases, what formulas might be used to help determine values, and what economic projections might affect a claim value. Each of these, while useful, must be balanced against the facts of the individual case, for no two major claims are identical.

Today even the settlement of injury claims can be accomplished by computer. Programs such as *CyberSettle®* offer insurers, defense, and plaintiff attorneys opportunities to negotiate over the Internet, with certain settlement parameters agreed to in advance. Such programs are perhaps a good twenty-first century addition to other forms of claim dispute resolution, such as mediation or arbitration. But like all methods of alternative dispute resolution, the key word is *alternative.* Such methods are alternatives to either practical and personal claim settlement negotiation or resolution in the courts.

> **Another Tool**
>
> *The computer is simply a tool. Like any tool it must be used carefully and correctly. Otherwise serious harm can occur.*

As the insurance industry comes to rely ever more heavily on the data provided by computer, it must always remember that the computer is simply a tool. Like any tool it must be used carefully and correctly. Otherwise serious harm can occur.

When is Litigating Unethical?

From a claim representatives' point of view, most litigation should be considered a failure to achieve the proper adjustment result. This is not to say that there should be no litigation of claims. Sometimes one side or the other becomes so entrenched in their position, or the loss factors involved are so complex or serious, that placing the matter before the court becomes the only sane thing to do.

As the New Jersey Supreme Court commented, "Although we encourage settlements, we recognize that litigants rely heavily on the professional advice of counsel when they decide whether to accept or reject offers of settlement, and we insist that the lawyers of our state advise clients with respect to settlements with the same degree of skill, knowledge, and diligence with which they pursue all other legal tasks. After all," adds the court, "*the negotiation of settlements is one of the most basic* and most frequently undertaken tasks that lawyers perform." (See *Ziegelheim v. Apollo, supra.,* 607 A.2d at 1304 [N.J., 1992].)

Proper handling of a claim is at the very least an ethical duty on the part of an insurer. For example, in the case of *Ranger County Mutl. Ins. Co. v. Guin,* 723 S.W.2d 656 (Texas 1987) the court commented that the "insurer's duty to its insured is not limited to . . . narrow boundaries . . . rather it extends to the full range of the agency [fiduciary?]

relationship." The court continued that this "includes investigation, preparation for defense of the lawsuit, trial of the case and reasonable attempts to settle."

One problem may be that too many claim departments do not allow their claim adjusters sufficient time to devote to dispute avoidance, with the result that litigation becomes an accepted method of resolving claims. An attitude of "fight every claim" is also present in many insurance companies and self-insured entities. Perhaps the notion that, faced with a minimal offer or the alternative of suing and undergoing the costly pressures of litigation, many third-party claimants—and even insureds—will accept the minimum offer and go away. Surprisingly, for many insurers and entities, this process seems successful. Ethically speaking, however, it may be minimally legal (if it does not violate the state's unfair claims settlement practice act) but morally obnoxious. Ultimately it wins neither the long-term battle nor the respect of the public toward such insurers or entities, and the entire industry suffers as a result.

Thought Provokers

1. Under what circumstances might an agent or broker be accused of having a conflict of interest?

2. In what ways might an insufficient investigation of a claim lead to allegations of bad faith?

3. What is the difference between being in charge and being in control?

4. Why is it not sufficient for a corporation or other entity to simply have a code of ethics without senior management support and frequent educational programs on the subject?

5. What are some differences between a personal code of ethics and an organization's code of ethics?

6. In regard to insurance claims, is there too much litigation or not enough litigation?

Chapter 7

The Hazards of Insurance Malpractice

"Why did the chicken cross the busy highway? Well, it failed to recognize the hazards!"

Anonymous Insurer Risk Manager

G ood ethics, like good health practices, requires a high degree of discipline. An unhealthy lifestyle including cigarettes, a high-fat high-caloric diet, immoderate alcohol consumption, and a lack of exercise inevitably will lead to health problems. Likewise, a bad attitude toward work, family, and society also will lead to mishaps and mayhem.

For the professional—any professional, whether engaged in a true profession as discussed in Chapter 2 or simply in a professional vocation such as insurance—bad habits and improper approaches to individual cases become exposures to malpractice. But just as eating one rich dessert does not bring on a heart attack, one breach of duty does not always result in a claim against a professional. Professions often involve trial and error: a physician cannot save every patient, nor can an attorney win every case.

When the error, however, was preventable and resulted in loss to the patient or client, there is inherent danger. We call this professional liability, malpractice, or errors and omissions (E&O). Annually, thousands of such claims are made against professionals in all ranks of life, including insurance agents, brokers, and adjusters. The ethical cause of much of this malpractice is bad habits and poor attitudes. Fortunately, this is a risk that can be managed.

Managing the insurance E&O exposure is similar to managing any risk. There are two sides to the formula: arranging to finance the losses (and there *will* be losses to pay) and controlling the losses both before and after they occur. The financial side of this formula can be handled in a combination of ways including paying out of pocket, funding the risk in either a formal or informal way, borrowing to pay the costs, or

Loss Control for E&O

After identifying what aspects of habit or attitude—our behavior patterns—can lead to mistakes, we can then do something about them. If we cannot eliminate them, we can perhaps reduce the exposure by modifying how we go about our business.

even declaring bankruptcy. A good portion of the costs can be transferred contractually, through either indemnification or hold harmless agreements or the mechanism of insurance.

The loss control side of the formula is more difficult. As with any aspect of risk control, the first step is identifying the hazards. After identifying what aspects of habit or attitude—our behavior patterns—can lead to mistakes, we can then do something about them. If we cannot eliminate them, we can perhaps reduce the exposure by modifying how we go about our business.

E&O: The Pickles and Jams of the Insurance Industry

Nobody likes to get sued or have a claim made against her. At one time it was so strongly believed that a physician would not be guilty of malpractice that a physicians' professional liability policy covered only the cost of defense—not payment of claims. These policies later were modified to pay judgments, but there usually was a clause that restricted the insurer from settling a claim without the physician's written consent. Now professional liability claims and judgments are rampant in all professions and professional vocations. "The field of professional liability defense is certainly growing," wrote Charles R. Norris, Chairman of the Defense Research Institute's Professional Liability Committee, in the December, 2000, issue of *For the Defense*. "More and more lawyers are defending other professionals, and there is an increasing need for an exchange of information on how to handle such claims."

Norris comments on a survey of the increasing exposure of insurance agents and brokers to professional liability. "This increase is due largely to the traditional agent's response to others' more aggressive promotion of low-cost insurance products, including use of the Internet. The agents have begun to bill themselves as insurance 'consultants' and 'professional advisors', and this has raised the standard of care expected of them." Regarding "the broadening field of financial services advisors," Norris adds, "[T]hey are required to report any claims against them to the appropriate governing body, and failure to do so could jeopardize their professional licenses."

Risk and claim managers not only coordinate insurance coverages, self-funded programs, and claims covering everything from fiduciary liability and fidelity bonds to property and casualty exposures. They also organize loss control processes ranging from auto safety programs and repetitive trauma exposures to international kidnapping. They are charged with resolving "corporate pickles and jams!"

Staying out of pickles and not stepping into mud-puddles or getting in a jam—whatever we call E&O mistakes and claims—are vitally important to any organization and professional person. It is too late to do much about such claims after the sheriff delivers a summons and complaint if the allegations are true. The time to prevent an E&O is before it happens.

Recognizing the Hazards

Only a handful of significant hazards underlay each and every professional E&O loss regardless of the profession involved. Most of the hazards cannot be eliminated entirely. They might be summed up in one significant twenty-first century hazard: lack of sufficient time to do the job right.

Where have we heard that before? "If you don't have the time to do it right the first time, how on earth are you going to find the time to do it over again?" This is a good question. In the 1980s time management became a popular topic, and entrepreneurs traveled the country, basically selling paper—paper that featured blanks for time scheduling. Much of this was a wonderful idea.

> **Time Is the Culprit!**
>
> *The significant hazards underlaying professional E&O losses might be summed up in one significant twenty-first century hazard: lack of sufficient time to do the job right.*

While some time-management plans are excellent, many have built-in flaws. For example, one time-management specialist suggested that business executives "throw away all the ads" and not take time to read them. Unfortunately, mailed notices of new products that might have benefited the organization got trashed as well. Another was "save nothing. Saving stuff only costs time and consumes space, and you'll never need it again." Oh yeah? You bet!

Some professional E&O hazards are common in all areas of the insurance industry, from claim adjusting to marketing and underwriting. At times, humor may be helpful in discussing them.

The Hazard of Careless Documentation

In Agatha Christie's Hercule Poirot mystery, *The Murder of Roger Ackroyd*, one character cites a quotation from Rudyard Kipling in describing a very nosey person: "The motto of the mongoose is 'Go and find out!'" For anyone who has ever seen a mongoose—a small, furry, ferret-like critter that charges along with its nose to the ground—the suggestion is apropos. But this also makes a good motto for those in the insurance industry. We must, if we are to act ethically and keep ourselves out of trouble, find out everything we need to know to do the task at hand correctly. Information, imagination, and ingenuity are aspects of ethics we have been exploring. Each requires positive action.

Careful and accurate documentation of factors affecting a decision is necessary. No physician can diagnose without examining; she cannot treat without diagnosing. If the examination is careless and misses some of the symptoms, the diagnosis will be incorrect, and the treatment may prove fatal. She cannot prescribe a medication without knowing all the benefits or contraindications of that medication and how it might react in a patient. Likewise, no attorney can properly defend or prosecute a case until he has all the facts and has researched the law.

It is no different in the insurance industry. Whether the professional is an agent helping a customer select an insurance policy or an adjuster handling a claim, careless documentation is a hazard. A simple mistake in evaluating coverage, a miscalculation of measurements in a property claim, or an overlooked statute illustrates the cliché that "haste makes waste!"

Careless Documentation

How can we manage the hazard of careless documentation?

As risk managers of our own loss exposures, how can we treat the hazard of careless documentation? We cannot actually eliminate it, and there is no easy way to transfer the hazard to someone else. The best we can hope for, therefore, is to reduce the hazard by first recognizing that it exists and then outlining the details in each situation that must be covered.

Checklists are available for agents and brokers to use when interviewing clients. They aid in gaining enough information to provide proper assistance. Careful review of the policy application, plus other information relating to the risk, should be mandatory.For those on the claims side of the business, many documentation tools are available. For example, the *Casualty, Fire & Marine Investigation Checklists, Fifth Edition,* published by West Group, contains twenty-seven chapters of detailed investigation and evaluation recommendations for virtually any type of nonlife or health insurance claim.

What else can we do to counter the hazard of careless documentation? One option is close supervision. No physician can simply graduate from medical school, hang up a plaque, and start practicing medicine. The same is true of pilots—soloing comes only after long and tedious study and practice with an instructor. Yet, in the insurance industry, we tend to believe that we simply can hire someone, teach him a few basics, and send him out on his own to do the job. To proceed without close supervision is simply unethical.

The Hazard of Bad Supervision

That supervision, however, must be good supervision. There are, throughout the insurance industry, many men and women who hold supervisory positions who know very little about the field in which they are engaged. Perhaps they have been employed ten years. This does not necessarily mean that they have had ten years experience in the industry—it may only mean that they have had one year's experience ten times!

Do You Agree?

Poor supervision may be just as bad as no supervision.

Modern business structure often results in the creation of slots. In a claims department, for example, the person in charge (perhaps the vice president of claims) may have slots for three claims managers, divided by line of coverage or by territory. Then there may be three slots under each manager for claim supervisors. Under each supervisor there may be six more slots for claim examiners, and then ten or twelve slots for adjusters or other claim representatives, with more boxes for support personnel, clerks, attorneys, appraisers, nurses, and other assistants. It is easy for the guy in the top box to move people from one slot to another, like chessmen on a game board. But just because someone fills a slot does not necessarily mean that he belongs in that particular box. As stated in the classic business text of the late 1960s, *The Peter Principle—Why Things Always Go Wrong*, (Morrow 1969), people tend to rise to a level of inefficiency and incompetence. "Occupational incompetence is everywhere," say the authors. They cite the cause as promotion of people who may be competent in one task to ever higher positions until they reach a level where they are incompetent—and that is where they stay!

What does this mean in terms of supervision? Within the insurance industry supervisory, managerial, and executive personnel must be knowledgeable about not only the insurance business but also about personnel management. John may be a great adjuster: very accurate, very precise, with an excellent settlement record and no complaints. He likes his job and does it well. Wouldn't John make a wonderful supervisor of five other adjusters?

> ### The Road to Success?
>
> *Americans seem to believe that, unless a person is promoted to a managerial or executive position, she is a failure. Perhaps we have it backwards, unless the manager or executive is both a skilled technician and a skilled people motivator. Few are.*

The answer is not necessarily yes. John may not be good at motivating others. He may not be able to delegate. Failure by a task-oriented supervisor or executive to delegate and rely on staff is a notorious cause of managerial mayhem.

It is one thing to be proficient at a task; it is quite another to mentor someone to become proficient at that task. Americans seem to believe that, unless a person is promoted to a managerial or executive position, she is a failure. We highly reward managers and executives and pay skilled workers far less. Perhaps we have it backwards, unless the manager or executive is both a skilled technician and a skilled people motivator. Few are. Failure follows.

Corporate downsizing, pay that does not entice qualified individuals to apply to and remain with the corporation after being hired, and promoting people who don't have sufficient education or experience to understand and be skilled at the job all contribute to E&O occurrences. It's perfectly legal, but awfully hazardous.

Are there any other ways to improve upon the dangers of poor supervision that leads to careless documentation? Education and training is one way. While book learning alone is insufficient to make a professional, experience alone, without the necessary academic endeavors and skill mentoring, inevitably will lead to loss. A well trained, educated, and supervised individual will recognize the need for accurate information for each task. That will go a long way toward avoiding the pitfalls of E&O.

The Hazard of Unclear Communication

Anyone who has ever attempted to decipher a government document or tried to program a video machine knows the hazards that unclear communication poses. Ambiguity in language always will work to the advantage of the other party.

> **"But you said . . ."**
>
> *What are the most dangerous three little words?*

What are the most dangerous three little words? They are three little words that will come to haunt whoever hears them. The sweat will pour, the collar tighten, and the hearer will know he is in deep trouble. They are, "But you said . . ."

It is the Information Age. Everywhere you look, someone is on the telephone, talking to someone, communicating. It's all words; someone is listening to those words that often constitute a promise. Eventually something will be said but misunderstood, and the other party will hear those three horrible words, "But *you said...*"!

> **Reducing the Hazard**
>
> *One way to reduce the hazard of unclear communication is to reduce the volume of oral communication involving important matters. Written communication is much safer than oral communication.*

If unclear communication is a hazard, what can we do about it? One way to reduce the hazard is to reduce the volume of oral communication involving important matters. Written communication (if the writer thinks before writing) is much safer than oral communication. By sending the original and keeping a copy, both sides will know exactly what was said, and, hopefully, what was meant. Email fits this criterion well, although it has its own built-in hazard. Email messages may be easily forwarded to others, and confidentiality may be lost. It also may be accidentally deleted. While the technology industry may be ready for a paperless society, professional loss control managers are not.

Unclear communication often can involve modern or technical terminology. Computerized shorthand may be used in messages and notes. This may involve the use of first names and jargon that may make the report meaningless when the information is needed. For example, a claim report might read, "The ee told Jane to f/u with the aa and Jane had Bill arng/ime." What does it mean? Who are Jane and Bill? If the matter goes to litigation and this notation is transcribed, it will be useless. Unclear communication is usually lazy communication.

The Hazard of Procrastination

One of the early "Iconoclast" columns, written nearly thirty years ago for the monthly publication of the South Florida Claims Association, was entitled *The Artful Use and Abuse of Procrastination*. "Is there any more hated aspect of human behavior than procrastination?", I asked. "If the 'wages of sin are death,' then the wages of procrastination must be lines—long lines at the end of the month when all the other procrastinators get together to do what ought to have been done at the beginning of the month. How we Americans hate lines—any kind of lines: bread lines, front lines, deadlines, dotted lines, red lines, bottom lines, headlines . . . "

Humor aside, procrastination is not just a hazard; it may be a useful tool. Like most tools, however, it must be used correctly. We must carefully select the tasks we can safely postpone and learn to not set aside the tasks that are necessary. Most people have more to do than time to do it. It is easy to take a list of things to do and to do the easy, quick items first, before tackling the important tasks. But then the phone rings, or something else comes up, and the important matter gets shoveled to the bottom of the stack.

Along with careless documentation, procrastination can be dangerous.

To illustrate, take the story of the lawsuit papers that just didn't make it to the top of anyone's list—until it was too late. A lawsuit involving a minor traffic accident should have received immediate attention from the insured, his agent, the insurance company claim department, and the adjuster. However, a series of delays and other priorities kept forcing it to the bottom of the pile. Before anyone took actiont, the plaintiff's attorney had filed for a default judgment and directed verdict, with a requested award of $1.2 million!

Serious Results

Procrastination can cause serious losses in many ways.

This is only one way in which procrastination can create a serious loss. Statutes of limitations constantly catch those involved in the insurance business in legal gotchas that can spring back in the form of E&O claims. Even states with long injury or damage statutes of limitations may have only a limited time statute if the loss involves a governmental agency. If the county's garbage truck smashes the insured's parked car, the subrogation cannot wait a year or so for collection.

Procrastination in submitting coverage applications to insurers also can create problems. If the agent has bound coverage, but the application and premium payment are delayed, the insurer knows nothing about the risk. If a loss occurs, that agent or broker may not be very popular with the underwriter.

Many insurance policies have built-in time factors. The insured must notify the company of losses or suits "promptly" or "as soon as practicable" or even "immediately." The policy may have a time limit after the loss for filing a proof of loss, and the company may have a stated obligation to respond to that within a certain number of days.

The 165-line *1943 New York Standard Fire Policy* format, still in use in many states, specifies that "The amount of loss for which this Company shall be liable shall be payable sixty days after proof of loss . . " Many states have tightened such time limitations. In Texas, for example, the claim must be paid within five days of having accepted proof of the loss.

The range of dates in which a lawsuit must be answered runs from fifteen days in Louisiana to thirty in California, with most at twenty or twenty-one days. There is no time to fool around; the insured may have procrastinated before notifying anyone about them. Default judgments are not always fatal; in many states the insurer loses only the right to dispute liability but may be able to dispute damages. But just because liability against an insured is clear, defaults should not be taken lightly.

Why do people procrastinate? There are many reasons. In most cases it is a matter of having too much to do and not enough time to do it. When any organization starts to become bogged down in problems resulting from employee procrastination, it may be the fault of senior management who have downsized or failed to hire enough people to handle the jobs correctly. Or it may be an individual problem with a particular employee.

Time a Factor

Why do people procrasti-nate? In most cases it is a matter of having too much to do and not enough time to do it.

One cause of procrastination, psychologists suggest, is perfectionism. A worker may want each job to be perfect and subsequently puts off the job until he believes he can do it perfectly. Another is fear—possibly related to fear that the job cannot be done perfectly and therefore won't be done at all. Fear of criticism from the boss also may cause of procrastination. Or, the boss wants his report, and it had better reflect good news. If the news is not good, however, the employee may delay providing the report. The hazard of procrastination—like business ethics in general—is often a top down problem. Unless there is commitment at the top of an organization to perform every task as soon as possible, procrastination will bog down the business like sludge in an automobile's engine.

The Hazard of Disorganization

The hazard of disorganization does not mean a cluttered desk. Disorganization is primarily a hazard for people in the claims business, although it also affects production, marketing, and underwriting.

The nine steps of the claim adjusting process consists of six main words: *investigation, evaluation,* and *negotiation* of the *coverage* first, then the *liability,* and finally the *damages.* For agents and brokers, the logical order might be to first analyze a customer's need; second, to determine necessary financial information such as how large a deductible the customer can bear; third, to determine which coverages best fit the customer's need; and finally, which insurer offers the best product for the need. Step by step, each process must be accomplished in its proper order. If steps are done out of order, chaos and an E&O claim can result.

Take the true story of Suzie, a claim adjuster who followed her company's motto, "We contact every claimant within twenty-four hours." Unfortunately, during that contact she negotiated the *damages* (the final step in the adjustment process) before investigating the *liability* (the fourth step). Suzie took the claimant's statement that she was the victim of Suzie's insured and authorized rental of a replacement vehicle and repair of the claimant's car. It later turned out that the claimant, and not Suzie's insured, had caused the accident.

The claimant sued Suzie and her employer-insurance company when they refused to pay the claim. The claimant alleged emotional distress, mental anguish, and $3,225 in damages resulting from promissory estoppel—the amount of the repair bill and car rental. The case went to trial with a demand for $300,000, and testimony went badly for Suzie. The jury was out for over an hour when defense counsel successfully negotiated a settlement of $57,000.

What went wrong? The hazard of disorganization led Suzie to make an unconditional offer to pay damages. The claimant accepted the offer. The claimant incurred repair and rental car bills because of the offer-acceptance, and she was damaged. She had acted in good faith and did what Suzie suggested. When Suzie and her employer reneged on the offer, the claimant sustained real loss.

The Hazard of Undisclosed Principalship

The insurance industry *represents*. It does things *on behalf of*. There are agents of the insurer and agents of the insured who deal with agents of other parties, perhaps attorneys representing claimants or corporate counsel representing parties to the policy. Insurers often represent other insurers. A primary insurer often represents an excess insurer in negotiations, and it also represents its own reinsurers in those negotiations. Who is representing whom should always be disclosed, but that does not always happen. Often the chain of representation is not known because of the way contracts are written.

Many times insurers have encountered serious legal situations created because some party failed to disclose their representation. When acting as an agent for someone else, we must disclose the identity of our principal. If there is more than one principal, we must disclose that, too. In insurance situations, we often represent many principals, and we must disclose each of them.

In a recent issue of *Claims* magazine, a reader challenged what the Iconoclast column had stated, that many third party claim administrators (TPAs) were really independent insurance adjusters. Referring to a high-deductible policy as opposed to a pure self-insurance program, the letter-writer said, "When we are functioning as that TPA, our allegiance and loyalty are to our client . . . as confirmed and approved by the carrier . . ." However, if there is a carrier, the insured, regardless of the amount of the deductible, is *not* that claim administrator's contract client, but, rather, its customer. The terms of the policy contract—regardless of the deductible—control the claim. This issue is discussed in Chapter 3.

That claim administrator represents his contract client—almost always the insurance company—but also represents the named insured. The TPA also represents the insurance company's reinsurers, the insured's excess insurers, and any additional insureds that are protected by the policy. Who on earth are all these principals, and how can we disclose them if we don't know who they are?

Failure to disclose the identity of our principals to parties with whom we are dealing is a hazard. In third-party claims, failing to include someone or some entity whose interest is also protected by the policy in a release may result in a serious E&O claim.

Corporate and other commercial insureds constantly are adding parties to their insurance coverages. These may be added by a specific endorsement to the policy—as loss payee, mortgagee, or additional insured—and represented on a certificate of insurance issued by the agent or broker. This is very common in connection with contracts such as leases, where the lease requires that the lessor be named an additional insured to the tenant's liability policy. When Carol falls down the stairs in a department store and breaks her arm, she's going to sue the landlord. Depending on how the lease is worded, the tenant's insurer may have to pay.

Insurance policies cover other interests regardless of whether or not the insurer knows about them. Auto policies, for example, provide coverage to persons using the insured's vehicle with the insured's permission—and even to such persons' own principals, usually an employer. If Joe borrows Sam's car to run an errand for Joe's boss and hits a pedestrian, Joe's boss becomes an insured of Sam's insurer—the boss's interest, as well as the interests of Joe and Sam, must be identified, disclosed to parties with whom the insurer deals, and protected in any settlement. To fail to do so could result in a bad faith claim against the insurer.

Likewise, if Kim takes out a second mortgage on her home, the loan company has an insurable interest in Kim's policy regardless of whether the insurer knows it is there or not. In the event of a loss, that relationship must be disclosed and protected.

The courts generally have been favorable to agents who have clearly disclosed their principalship, even when they have exceeded their limited authority. A South Carolina court commented that "the record discloses that (the defendant adjusters) as agents for a disclosed principal were acting for and on behalf of the insurers, and therefore may not be held responsible for the liability incurred." (*Falcon Flying Services v. McKamey*, 193 So.2d 402 [La. 1966].) In the Pennsylvania case of *Huddock v. Donegal Mutl. Ins. Co.*, 246 A.2d 668 (1970) the court dismissed the adjusters, ruling that "actions by the adjusters beyond the scope of their authority could not result in the imposition upon them of contractual duties to the appellants which they had never assumed. The adjusters had a duty to their principals, the insurance companies, to perform whatever tasks were assigned them, but this duty did not create a contractual obligation between the adjusters and appellants." However, an Oregon court found that if an adjuster authorizes repairs without disclosing the name of his principal, he could be held contractually liable to the repairer if the principal fails to pay. (*Norswing v. Lakeland Flying Service,* 237 P.2d 586 [1951].)

> **Exceeding Authority**
>
> *The courts generally have been favorable to agents who have clearly disclosed their principalship, even when they have exceeded their limited authority.*

The situation in which this hazard is most evident is in allegations of an authorization or guarantee. An agent or broker *guarantees* that a client is covered for certain risks but fails to identify the insurance company that will write the coverage; if a loss occurs and the insurer denies coverage, the agent or broker may have to pay. If, on the other hand, an agent discloses that a particular insurance company's policy provides certain coverage, that principal may have to pay the claim, even if there is no such coverage under the policy; the agent has bound the principal by disclosure. Of course, the principal may have a right of action back against the agent, but that's a different situation!

An example of the role that improper authorizations or guarantees can have on a situation involves an independent adjuster, Bob Jackson. Right before a long weekend, Bob receives a call from a dispatcher for a trucking company insured by one of Bob's clients. The dispatcher reports a tanker accident, which includes a hazardous material spill. The dispatcher tells Bob that his company carries a $100,000 combined single limit auto policy, which includes pollution coverage.

Bob directs a pollution-cleanup company to the scene and starts home. On the drive he stops by the accident—which is surrounded by emergency vehicles—and talks to a representative of the cleanup company. After hearing that the cleanup crew usually disposes of hazardous wastes in the city dump, he authorizes the company to dump the material from the accident there.

Unfortunately for Bob and his company, the cleanup bill amounts to more than $2.3 million! And that does not include the bill from the federal Environmental Protection Agency for oversight and possible penalties. Should the insurance company send a check for the policy limits—$100,000? Who will pay the rest? And who will pay the bill for dumping hazardous material in the city dump, which subsequently was declared a Superfund site?

What happened? A simple hazard led to a disastrous financial situation. Bob neglected to disclose that he was just a limited agent; he forgot to disclose his principal to those with whom he dealt. In effect, he got hooked for *being in charge* when he should not even have been *in control* of the situation. He had contracted for and authorized work without any thought of how much would be involved or who should authorize such activities. He had not even investigated the *coverage*, the first step in the adjustment process—all he knew was what the dispatcher told him. Yet there he was, negotiating *damages*, the last step.

Good Advice

Do not address the loss without addressing the claim!

Bob addressed the loss without addressing the claim—all the things we have discussed in this book. Could things have worked out differently if Bob had suggested to the dispatcher that it was the insured who needed to authorize the pollution cleanup? Would the result have been different if Bob had clearly advised the pollution engineer that he was only a limited agent for the insurer and not authorized to sign anything? Was there unclear communication and disorganization in the adjustment steps when Bob said, "sounds okay to me" to the question of where to dump the pollutants?

This was a disaster, the kind of catastrophic loss that calls upon the skills of agents and adjusters in the way a Carnegie Hall performance calls upon the talents of a musician. Like the chicken that crossed the busy highway, Bob had failed to recognize hazards.

Bad Attitudes and Obnoxious Habits

It should be obvious that any bad habit and poor attitude toward the job, the town, the boss, the family, and life in general is hazardous as it relates to one's relationship to the insurance industry. This is where the concept of integrity becomes important. Someone with a poor attitude toward her home and family is probably going to carry that same attitude toward her professional life as well.

From Home to Career

Someone with a poor attitude toward her home and family is probably going to carry that same attitude toward her professional life as well.

This is more than a matter of politics, religion, and good health habits. Someone who is habitually angry, who has a volatile temper, is not only acting immaturely; that person is going to mouth off to some client or customer and be sued for slander or defamation. A man who acts inappropriately toward women is going to find himself explaining his over-active hormones to the judge in a sexual-harassment claim. Some eager-beaver claim representative who sees illegality, immorality, and criminal intent in every claim eventually will accuse the wrong person and be sued for malicious prosecution. It's all a matter of attitude and habits. When a life-style become hazardous, it is time to take action.

Thought Provokers

1. Make a list of ten factors related to your particular job where a lack of careful documentation could create a loss. For each, list two or more actions that might help to prevent a mistake.

2. Think back to the last time someone said, "But you said . . ." Did you say it? If you didn't, can you prove you didn't? Did you mean it the way the person interpreted it? How could you have said it differently so that it might not have been misunderstood?

3. For your state or jurisdiction (and for those in cities bordering on one or more other states those as well) make a list showing:

a. The number of days between the service of a lawsuit and when an answer is due;

b. The statute of limitations on a bodily injury claim, a property damage claim, a medical malpractice claim, and a claim against a governmental agency;

c. Any state insurance regulations relating to the time limit for payment of claims.

4. Consider the last five files handled (marketing, underwriting, or claims). Identify the persons or entities whose interests may be protected by the policy in addition to the named insured.

Chapter 8
The Perils of Errors and Omissions

"Ethos is your personal credibility, the faith people have in your integrity and competency. It's the trust that you inspire, your Emotional Bank Account. Pathos is the empathetic side—it's the feeling. It means that you are in alignment with the emotional thrust of another's communication. Logos is the logic, the reasoning part of the presentation."

Stephen R. Covey
The Seven Habits of Highly Effective People

Just as no single hazard is the actual cause of loss but only a contributing factor, most loss is the result of a combination of hazards. The loss itself is produced by the peril, the triggering mechanism of loss. Gasoline is hazardous, but it is not fire. Matches are hazardous, but they are not fire. A lighted match together with gasoline, however, produces explosion and fire.

In this chapter we look at some specific peril mechanisms that lead to E&O losses and suggest ways to avoid the pitfalls. These are mistakes that could be made by agents or brokers, underwriters, company or independent claim adjusters, or attorneys. While most relate to the claims side of insurance, many agents and brokers become actively involved in their customers' claims and need to be aware of such situations.

Failing to Know the Risk

A number of agent's E&O claims arise strictly out of the agent's failure to understand the risk. Whether the customer is an individual or a corporation, the agent or broker has an ethical duty to identify the potential exposures and at least discuss them with the customer. A checklist often is helpful, for it later can be used to demonstrate that the subject was discussed and coverage declined. But even when risk is properly assessed, the product recommended or sold must be the right product for the exposure.

Selling the Wrong Product

For example, while working as a corporate risk manager for an international risk

Stay Out of Trouble

The agent or broker has an ethical duty to identify the potential exposures and at least discuss them with the customer.

management and insurance services company that depended on its computers, I often was asked what type of computer business interruption coverage we carried. Many people were surprised when I said that we didn't carry any at all. We could not stop our business! Thousands of checks were issued weekly, for example, to workers compensation and other claimants. Imagine the litigation if we sent a letter that said, "We're terribly sorry, but our mainframe burned up last week, and we can't send you a compensation check for a couple of months."

What we did have was a combination of indirect loss coverages, such as expediting expense for our computer systems to cover the extra costs of obtaining immediate repair and replacement. We used this in combination with storing duplicates of our data off-site and contractual arrangements with a computer hot site, a standby facility with matching computing capabilities that we could use if necessary. We even had a standby power system. The program was carefully worked out between the information resources division executives, the risk management department, the broker, and the insurance company. Our insurer was so impressed with the system that it filmed a documentary of our state-of-the-art data processing center and risk management plan.

Business interruption coverage would have been the wrong product for our company. Conversely, for a business such as a small retail shop, business income coverage would be appropriate. Insurance is not a one-size-fits-all product. While some companies, agents, and brokers sell only off-the-rack coverages, those that are more successful are like fine tailors. They measure the customer, note his dimensions, and offer a variety of materials; they cut and trim a bit, then remeasure and cut some more, stitching here and there until the suit fits the customer exactly, is comfortable, serviceable, and correct. Often it may not be much more expensive than some droopy thing off the rack.

The Insured's Responsibilities

But just as the agent or broker has a duty to inquire about the insured's needs, the insured has an equal obligation to both explain his needs and to review the policy when it is received. In the New Jersey case of *Aden v. Fortsh,* 743 A.2d 371 (2000) the insured asked his auto insurance agent to procure coverage on his condominium.

The agent later testified that the insured said he wanted only minimum coverage, but the insured denied that. The policy that was issued provided only $1,000 for damage to the interior. When the insured sustained a $20,000 interior fire loss, he sued the agent. Dispute arose over whether the trial court should be allowed to consider the comparative negligence of the insured for failure to read the policy when he received it, and the matter ended up in the appellate court. Citing an earlier case, *Dancy v. Popp,* 556 A.2d 312 (1989), the court agreed that, absent any misrepresentation by the agent, the insured had a duty to read the policy.

However, in *Butcher v. Truck Ins. Exch.,* 92 Cal.Rptr.2d 521 (2000) a California court ruled that the insured's failure to read his policy did not preclude the insured's action for negligent misrepresentation against the agent who was to procure coverage identical to that of an expiring policy from a different insurer. The expiring, nonrenewed policy contained personal injury coverage, which the replacement policy did not. When the insured became embroiled in unsuccessful litigation, he was sued for malicious prosecution and found he had no coverage. The Court cited the *Restatement (2ⁿᵈ) of Torts, §551,* imposing "a duty to exercise reasonable care to disclose to the other before the transaction is consummated {¶} ... (e) facts basic to the transaction, if he knows that the other is about to enter into it under a mistake as to them, and that the other, because of the relationship between them, the customs of the trade or other objective circumstances, would reasonably expect a disclosure of those facts."

In one Maryland case an agent unsuccessfully appealed a decision that he had negligently failed to procure insurance on the basis that there had been no expert testimony on the standard of care owed by an agent and that the insured had failed to read the policy. The case involved territorial use warranties in a marine policy of Eastport, Maine, to Key West, Florida. (*CIGNA Prop. & Cas. Co. v. Zeitler,* 730 A.2d 248 [1998].)

In another type of case, the Arkansas Supreme Court, in the case of *Mashburn v. Meeker,* 5 S.W.3d 469 (1999) ruled that, because the insurer paid the full amount of claim despite the agent's negligent error in the binder regarding the route of navigation, the insured sustained no damage and could not bring a claim. Nevertheless, it pays to be accurate.

Other Procurement Issues

Many lawsuits have been brought against agents who have procured coverage for customers with insurers that later went bankrupt. In most cases the courts have found that the agent owes no duty to notify the insured in such a situation. Even though it may not be a legal duty, there may be an ethical duty for an agent to notify customers if an insurer with whom she has placed coverage becomes—or may become—insolvent. This is a wise business decision because, if for nothing else, the insured will need to replace the uncollectible coverage.

> **Minimum Standard Only**
>
> *Even if the courts find that the agent does not have a legal duty to advise customers regarding the adequacy of their coverages, there may be an ethical duty to do so. Law is the minimum duty owed; ethics is the highest.*

Likewise, even if the courts find that the agent does not have a legal duty to advise customers regarding the adequacy of their coverages, there may be an ethical duty to do so. As stated previously, law is the minimum duty owed; ethics is the highest.

In most jurisdictions the courts have held that an agent or broker does not owe a duty to a third party when there is no contractual duty. If an insured has insufficient coverage to indemnify a third-party victim of the insured's negligence, the injured party has no right of action against the agent. There are exceptions, however. In the case of *Alaniz v. Simpson,* 70 Cal. Rptr.2d 923 (1998) the fourth California appellate court in an unpublished case ruled that an insurance agent did owe a duty to third-party victims of an uninsured driver not to mislead that driver into believing he had coverage when he did not. Courts also have ruled that an agent's oral representation that coverage is provided by a policy when it is not does not modify the policy.

Coverage Errors

Joseph Pulitzer, the king of newspaper publishers, is reputed to have said that the three most important things in journalism are "accuracy, accuracy, and accuracy." The three most important aspects of real estate are "location, location, and location." Well, for those in the insurance business, the three most important things are "coverage, coverage, and coverage." In insurance, coverage is the key to everything. It is the vital key to selling and marketing, to underwriting, and to settling claims. Our understanding of coverage as it applies to each risk and loss must be accurate. Mistakes are costly. They are unforgiving and unforgivable.

> **Coverage Is the Key**
>
> *For those in the insurance business, the three most important things are "coverage, coverage, and coverage." In insurance, coverage is the key to everything.*

As noted previously, an agent or broker selling the wrong coverage for the risk can result in an E&O claim. Telling someone there is coverage when there is not may have been excused by the courts in a few cases cited, but there is at the least a moral duty to get it right and not mislead the customer.

Every aspect of coverage—from each individual factor in the declarations to the terms and conditions and endorsements—must be carefully analyzed and considered.

Nowhere is this more true than in the case of claim adjusting. The adjuster always must understand the loss; however, to adjust the claim—the financial contract demand—he first must ascertain the coverage. The slightest mistake can be costly.

Many in the industry believe that, after a year or so, they know all there is to know about coverage. We see the same situations over and over, and in most cases we probably are guessing correctly. But policy language constantly is changed to fit changing court interpretations or to fit new needs. The ISO commercial general liability (CGL) form has fourteen exclusions in it. Try to list them without looking. The personal auto policy has forty-six exclusions. Try listing those! In addition, each may have been modified by court decisions that could differ between states or jurisdictions within a state.

To illustrate the point, when is a claim *made* under a claims-made CGL form? Is it when the alleged loss happened, when the insured first has knowledge that there may be a loss, the date when someone writes to the insured asserting a claim, the date the insured gets that letter, the date a lawsuit is filed, or the date the lawsuit is served? Many are surprised to learn of the double trigger for that date. The policy states that a claim "will be deemed to have been made at the earlier of the following times: 1) When notice of such claim is *received* and *recorded* [two separate factors] by any insured or by us, whichever comes first; or 2) When we make settlement in accordance with (Insuring Agreement 1.a.) above." So, what happens if a claim is received on one day in one policy period but not recorded until a few days later in a different policy period? Coverage is not easy to understand!

Waiver & Estoppel

Most coverage errors that result in E&O claims arise from the legal principle of waiver and estoppel. An insured reports a claim; no one suggests that there is no coverage for it. The insured proceeds as if coverage applies and later discovers that there is no coverage. Because of her action or inaction, the matter has deteriorated. In such a situation the insurer may be *estopped* (prevented) from denying coverage.

Simply stated, the rule is this: If one party has a legal right but conveys an impression to a second party that it is not going to assert that legal right, and the second party acts upon that impression to his detriment, then the party who had the legal right may be prevented from asserting it.

Not all mistakes are fatal under this rule. An insured may have a water damage loss, for example, and both the agent and the insurer's adjuster may convey the impression that it will be covered—perhaps by writing an estimate of the damage. If it later is determined that there is no coverage, a denial may survive. Why? Even if the insured relied upon the impression conveyed by the agent and the adjuster that the loss would be covered, his repairing the damage was not detrimental to him. He would have had to repair the damage anyway. He may be upset with the insurer and the agent for their breach of the duty owed to him, but that negligence was not the proximate cause of his loss. The water damage itself was the cause of loss.

The situation was different in the case cited in Chapter 7 of Suzie and the at-fault claimant. That particular case was subject to Missouri law, which is typical regarding estoppel. In that case the claimant did rely on Suzie's statements to her detriment. The defendants argued that the claimant would have had to fix the car anyway, but it was likely that the jury would not have accepted that notion.

Actions taken to one's detriment as a cause of estoppel is not always the case, however. In *Lloyd's, etal. v. Fulton,* 2 P.3d 1199 (2000) the Alaska Supreme Court ruled that the insurers' failure to notify the insured of potential coverage defenses before obtaining statements from the insured (a reservation of rights letter was not sent to the insured until three weeks after the investigation began), estopped the insurers from asserting their coverage defenses. This was the case even though the failure had not really cost the insured any more than would have been lost had he known there was no coverage.

In every claim the adjuster must proceed as if the case for and against coverage were being prepared for trial. She must answer the question, "What would a judge and jury make of these facts?" If there is the slightest doubt of whether coverage applies, the investigation must be stopped until the problem is either resolved or the insured

> **Stay Out of Trouble**
>
> *In every claim the adjuster must proceed as if the case for and against coverage were being prepared for trial.*

has been placed on notice of the problem. With a third-party claim, the adjuster must not convey the impression that everything is fine if there are doubts about either coverage or the liability of the insured for it. A court may rule that comments that could be interpreted by a third party as an offer to settle constitute a contractual promise, the breach of which may result in an allegation of promissory estoppel.

> **Stop if in Doubt!**
>
> *If there is the slightest doubt of whether coverage applies, the investigation must be stopped until the problem is either resolved or the insured is placed on notice of the problem.*

Other types of problems also may arise. In one Illinois case in federal court, the Seventh Circuit ruled that an insurer that fails to provide an effective defense to the point that the insured's interests are prejudiced may be estopped from asserting coverage defenses, even though it had issued a reservation of rights. (*Willis Coroon Corp. v. Home Ins. Co.,* 203 F.3d 449 [7th Cir. 2000].)

Contractual Errors and Defects

Few insurance problems are as complex or difficult to resolve as those relating to contractual agreements between various parties that may affect the coverage. As discussed earlier, many insureds enter into a variety of contractual agreements with customers, clients, landlords, and others with whom they do business. In a construction wrap-up program, for example, a developer or general contractor may hold the threads of insurance coverages for all the subcontractors and suppliers. These agreements are extremely complex, put together by teams of lawyers who specialize in such deals. They often require the courts to interpret areas of dispute. If the agent, broker, underwriter, or claim representative fails to take all aspects of such contractual agreements into account—including the factoring in of any applicable statutes or court decisions—a costly error is likely to occur.

In the case of insureds and additional insureds, the actual insurance policy may not tell the entire story. The CGL policy, for example, takes more than one page to explain "Who Is an Insured." To fully understand the conditional factors it is necessary to understand the policy definitions. What is an "insured contract", for example? Who is a "leased worker", and how does he differ under the policy from a "temporary worker"? Many parties also may be shown as insureds when the agent or broker issues a certificate of insurance.

Cases abound where insurers have acted incorrectly regarding contracts and additional insureds. It is one of the most common areas of insurance litigation. Many of these involve employment-related claims by the employees of an additionally insured subcontractor against the general contractor or an additionally insured owner. Rules regarding such claims often differ by state. Other cases arise out of situations such as primary/excess coverage, inadequate limits of liability, failure of the additional insured to comply with policy conditions, and cross-liability actions between two or more insureds.

Many issues arise over whether a party added as an additional insured on a liability policy is covered for its own negligence or only for the negligence of the named insured. In the California case of *Acceptance Ins. Co. v. Syufy Enterprises,* 81 Cal. Rptr.2d 557 (1999), the appellate court interpreted the additional insured endorsement in a contractor's policy to provide coverage for the additionally insured owner's own independent negligence. However, if the policy is worded to exclude coverage for an additional insured's own negligence, as was stated to be Texas law in the case of *BP Chemicals Inc. v. First State Ins. Co.,* 226 F.3d 420 (6th Cir. 2000), then coverage will be barred for any claim alleging even partial negligence of that additional insured as contributing to a loss.

A slightly different circumstance was involved in another California case, *National Union Fire Ins. Co. v. Nationwide Ins. Co.,* 69 Cal. App.4th 709 (1999). In this case the appellate court ruled that an additional insured endorsement that extended coverage to liability that arose out of the general contractor's "general supervision" of the subcontractor did not apply to a premises defect caused solely by the named insured contractor. Each situation depends on the circumstances involved.

In one New Jersey case, a public entity that was an additional insured on a general contractor's policy was found to be covered for a personal injury claim by a subcontractor's employee who was injured while on the additional insured's premises to obtain information for a bid. (*County of Hudson v. Selective Ins. Co.*, 752 A.2d 849 [2000].)

Disputes also can arise when the named insured in a liability policy has a high deductible that also is applicable to additional insureds. In the case of *Northbrook Ins. Co. v. Kuljian Corp.*, 690 F.2d 368 (3rd Cir. 1982), the additional insured was insolvent when the insurer settled a claim against that negligent additional insured. The insurer then brought suit against the named insured to collect the deductible.

Authorizations and Guarantees

A pollution claim that got out of hand was introduced in Chapter 7. As illustrated in that example, agents and adjusters must be cautious about authorizing repairs or guaranteeing payments. When a limited agent fails to disclose that limited relationship and the identity of the principal, the courts will hold the agent responsible for the costs. This is a common problem, especially in first-party claims.

As stated previously, there is a difference between being in charge and being in control. The adjuster or agent may need to be in control of the claim to a certain degree, but the insured or third-party claimant is in charge of the repair, replacement, or treatment that may be needed. To do otherwise may result in an E&O claim in the making.

There are situations, however, in which the insurer does have a right under the policy to repair or replace damaged or stolen property as it so desires. Few insurers elect to enforce this contractual tool, however, for once the insurer undertakes a repair it is obligated to complete it to the insured's satisfaction. The same is true when replacing property—not only must it be of like kind and quality, but it must be a fair replacement.

One risk management tool that may be useful in preventing these types of problems is to print a legal notice on all appraisal forms. Such a notice places all parties on notice that the appraisal is simply that and does not constitute an offer, authorization to repair, or guarantee of payment. Only the

Risk Management Tool

The legal principle that a written notice takes precedence over an oral statement may be used to eliminate some types of E&O claims.

owner, the notice should state, can do that. Regardless of what the appraiser might say, the legal principle that a written notice takes precedence over an oral statement may eliminate this type of E&O claim.

Failure to Protect All Interests

Usually a result of the careless documentation hazard, an E&O claim alleging failure to protect someone's interest in a settlement can be costly. Such failures can arise in either first- or third-party claims either in the way a liability release or a settlement check is drawn. Allegations of failing to protect all interests can result from a number of interests, such as:

1. Loss payees or mortgagees, whether or not they are shown on the policy. For example, many condominium association by-laws require that the association carry insurance on the common areas. The by-laws usually specify a particular officer or individual as the recipient of insurance benefits. If an adjuster simply issues the check to the named insured association without specifying the particular recipient, and the money is placed in the general fund and not allocated for repairs, the insurer may become liable to the association for shortfall in repair payments. In Florida, for example, insurers must include loan institutions on any first- or *third*-party settlement involving an automobile that is used as collateral for a loan.

2. Parties with an insurable interest in insured property. Such interests generally are protected to whatever extent the policy specifies. If the insurer settles only with the named insured, those parties may have a right of action against the insurer.

3. Lienholders. This may include a repair facility, a medical-services provider, or other parties with a financial interest in the settlement.

4. A legal representative. This may include parents or guardians of minors, executors of estates, trustees, an appointed recipient for a condominium association, or any party identified to the insurer as the party authorized to receive the funds. The most common situation is an attorney representing an insured or third-party claimant, and, in first-party cases, a public adjuster.

5. Any additional insured or party entitled to coverage or protection under the policy.

6. The subrogation interests of an insurer that has paid its insured and is entitled to recovery from a tortfeasor.

In most cases, the easiest way to protect all qualified parties is to include all the names on the settlement check. Even though this may be cumbersome, it avoids having to sort out who is entitled to what, especially when the settlement is for less (due to deductibles, limits of liability, comparative negligence offsets, or other insurance applicable to the claim) than the loss amount. A check with numerous payees may cause problems for the recipients, but the endorsement of each interest protects the insurance company. The insured, the claimant, or their legal counsel will be in charge of getting the endorsements, not the insurer.

Where the parties cannot agree on distribution—as in a policy limits case in which there are more claimants than settlement funds—another means of protecting interests is to pay the money into a court for distribution. The rules for this differ among jurisdictions, but in most cases the court will take jurisdiction, approving the settlement and distributing the funds.

Spoliation of Evidence

A relatively new tort, not yet recognized as actionable in some states, is that of *spoliation* of evidence. It is now common for those in the claims business, either insurers or independent adjusters, to be accused of spoliation whenever physical evidence is lost or rendered useless.

This can happen directly or indirectly. In one such case an employee was seriously injured because of the alleged malfunction of a valve on a piece of equipment. The insured employer had the valve and took it out of service because of the alleged malfunction. The workers compensation insurer retained a firm to examine it for subrogation possibilities. That firm did so but did not take possession of it. When one of the insured's employees asked what to do with the valve, the examiner replied, "Well, I've seen it." So it was thrown out. The injured employee brought suit against the valve manufacturer but, without the valve, he could not prove either the malfunction nor that the defendant manufacturer had made the valve. Therefore he also sued his employer, the workers compensation insurer, and the outside firm for spoliation of the evidence.

A similar situation involved a cable used to restrain a dog that broke and allowed the dog to attack the plaintiff. The insurer took possession of the cable but then lost it. The Indiana Court of Appeals authorized a spoliation claim against the insurer for its failure to preserve evidence. (*Thompson v. Owensby, et al.,* 704 N.E.2d 134 [1998].)

Whenever evidence is either lost or in some manner rendered valueless, the damage is not just the value of the actual piece of evidence. The value is what the evidence represents, what someone might collect in a negligence case against the maker of the evidence.

Mathematical Errors

While insurance marketing, underwriting, and claims are primarily a *word* business, numbers are very important. Serial numbers must be recorded correctly. Dates of birth, dates of treatment, dates of purchase, or dates of loss are all vitally important. We cannot guess at factors such as age, value, size, length, or width. They must be exact.

Anyone who has been involved in the calculation of a retrospectively rated policy knows how important numbers are. Without stating the retrospective formula here, both the amount of the premium base and the incurred loss amount must be correct. The method of calculation must be precise. The ethics of correct calculation are as important as in any other aspect of insurance. Putting inaccurate factors into a customer's premium is as unethical as a butcher putting his thumb on the scale as he weighs the lamb chops.

Mismanaging Medical Care or Repairs

The volume of litigation against insurers that operate HMOs continues to grow. While most actions are subject to ERISA and the federal courts, new inroads by state jurisdiction occur monthly. A federal court in Pennsylvania ruled that ERISA preempts state law claims arising from an HMO's refusal to authorize treatment, but a Texas federal court ruled that accusations against an HMO for creating financial incentives that discouraged proper medical testing were not subject to total preemption by ERISA. (*Cyr v. Kaiser Foundation Health Plan of Texas,* 12 F.Supp.2d 556 [1998].) An HMO can also be sued under a breach-of-contract theory for failure to provide quality care, a Connecticut court ruled in *Natale v. Meia,* No. 96005491S, 1998 Conn. Super. LEXIS 1230 (April 30, 1998).

> **New Source of Lawsuits**
>
> *The volume of litigation against insurers that operate HMOs continues to grow.*

Analysis of recent cases shows that courts and juries are becoming less tolerant of managing care from a distance, where clerks rely upon computers to authorize treatment. Patients can pay for what the doctor orders on their own, but limitations by insurers may bar that option because of cost. Physician appeals seem an odd requirement for what may be an urgent matter.

Just as insurers have been sued for mandating the use of aftermarket auto parts to repair collision damage, medical insurers have been sued for bad results of utilization review and other medical cost-containment procedures. However, in many cases the insurers were dismissed, simply because the law places the ultimate burden of responsibility for the patient's care on the physician, not the insurer. In one of the earliest managed care challenges, *Wickline v. State of California,* 727 P.2d 753 (1986), the appellate court held that it was the duty of the physician to mandate the appropriate care. Although this case subsequently was superseded by a grant of review and depublished, it illustrates some of the issues surrounding this type of situation. The plaintiff had been hospitalized and had some complications. The physician recommended that she be kept in the hospital longer than California's Medicaid utilization panel permitted. The physician acquiesced, and the patient was discharged. At home the wound became infected, gangrene set in, and the patient had to be returned to the hospital where her leg was amputated. She sued the insurer and its utilization review provider, alleging that they were responsible because they would not authorize a longer hospital stay. The courts found otherwise.

The next major challenge also occurred in California. In *Wilson v. Blue Cross of So. Cal.,* 222 Cal. App. 3d 660 (1990), the physician hospitalized the patient for a month for depression. The insurer's utilization reviewers would authorize only ten days of hospitalization, so the patient was discharged after only ten days. Three weeks later he committed suicide. His estate sued the insurer. While the trial court dismissed the action based on *Wickline,* on appeal the Second Appellate District Court rejected that theory and raised issues of whether a private insurer or utilization review firm could be held liable for the harm resulting from cost-containment procedures, returning the case to the trial court.

To further complicate the situation, a Wyoming court in *Long v. Great West Life & Annuity Ins. Co.,* 957 P.2d 823 (1998) found that a health-plan administrator could be sued for damages resulting from a utilization-review decision, but a federal court in Massachusetts ruled that ERISA preempted a similar action. (*Danca v. Emerson Hospital,* 9 F.Supp.2d 27 [1998].)

Is there a potential conflict of interest when an insurer or related firm attempts to manage a patient's care or a claimant's property repairs? In an address to the American Society of Healthcare Risk Management in October of 1996, Dr. Robert E. Pendrak, vice president and medical director of PHICO Group, a Pennsylvania insurer, commented that managed care, including incentives to physicians to limit expenses, could create conflict. "A physician's financial reward versus a physician's moral/ethical responsibilities to the patient may be compromised," he said.

As expensive twenty-first century technology becomes more available, patients' needs, physicians' desires, and insurers' mandates inevitably will clash.

Nevertheless, America still has one of the better medical systems in the world. It is expensive, and the health-insurance industry would be unethical if it did not act to contain unreasonable costs in all possible ways. Most of us know of someone who has grossly abused the medical system through over-utilization. Over-medicating is nearly a national epidemic. Shouldn't someone take control of this misuse? Of course. But the "them" of managed care ultimately is "us."

Mismanaging Property-Related Claims

While auto repair parts were gaining headlines at the end of the twentieth century, disputes over property-related claims have hogged the insurance and litigation news for centuries. Few topics can generate a debate faster than that of valuation of property and coverage issues. To its credit, the insurance industry has employed many contractual tools to make insurance equitable for both the insurer and the insured, procedures such as coinsurance clauses, replacement cost coverage, sublimits on high-value items that should be insured elsewhere, and the steady addition of indirect, contingent, and consequential loss coverages to standard policies.

Valuation disputes often arise over matters such as the definition of *actual cash value* (ACV). Is it really the cost of repair or replacement with like kind and quality, less physical depreciation and obsolescence, or is it fair market value under the Broad Evidence Rule, a diminution of value, or some other measurement? James J. Markham, J.D., CPCU, states in an Insurance Institute of America text that "Determining the actual cash value of a repair estimate requires a knowledge of the useful life of building components as well as the court decisions dealing with ACV in the jurisdiction. Most policies do not define the term." He adds, "Regardless of the definition of ACV, depreciation is warranted only when repairs leave the insured in a better situation than he or she was in before the loss.... Determining the ACV involves examining each item of repair and quantifying the extent of betterment [considering the] age, condition and expected use of the item...."

In Volume I of the text, Markham spends nearly an entire chapter discussing how to calculate depreciation of personal property. He cites a number of possible calculation methods that can be used depending on the type of item. With all these possibilities and inexactitudes, is it any wonder that disputes arise over the value of used underwear, broken dishes, smashed furniture, and water-soaked books?

Many adjusters take relatively little time or energy to evaluate personal property claims accurately. They are prone to apply some sort of charted straight-line depreciation factor across the board on a take it or leave it basis, trusting that the calculation may be high on some items, low on others, and just right on one or two. On average, it may work. But is that ethical? Is it the kind of adjusting that can set the adjuster up for a lawsuit?

Do You Agree?

Like litigation, the appraisal process represents a failure of the adjuster to negotiate properly from the basis of proper investigation and evaluation.

Most would say no, reminding a threatening insured of the appraisal clause in the policy. But like litigation, the cumbersome and often arbitrary appraisal process represents a failure of the adjuster to negotiate properly from the basis of proper investigation and evaluation.

Often, typical property coverage disputes arise out of definitions of perils. While there is not too much argument over the difference between friendly and hostile fire, changes in many standard personal and commercial lines property forms over the definition and coverage for collapse often leave insureds and their insurers at odds. For example, when a serious impairment of the structural integrity of a roof led to the closing of a nursing home in Pennsylvania, leading to a business interruption claim for collapse, the Third Circuit Court of Appeals ruled that, under Pennsylvania's law, this was not "collapse." (*Meritcare Inc. v. St. Paul Mercury Ins. Co.,* 166 F.3d 214 [3rd Cir. 1998].)

Another troublesome area involves water damage. Most standard commercial and personal property insurance policies exclude various types of flood damage, including backup of sewers. A plumbing overflow, however, generally is covered. To backup, as in "I backed up in my driveway," means to move in a backward direction. Sewage overflows usually occur because of a blockage with more material being added behind the blockage until it overflows. Only occasionally are such losses caused by an actual reverse flow, which might be caused by either a sewage pump malfunction, or by flooding conditions where the blockage of one sewer line causes the sewage to flow in an opposite direction (reverse flow) down an intersecting line. Yet adjuster after adjuster denies coverage based on sewer backup when it was probably only an overflow from within the insured's own plumbing system.

Do You Agree?

If insurers and their claim representatives are going to avoid disputes with their own insureds over coverage, they have to be extremely careful in their analysis of the claim. Far too many like to move to the third step, negotiation or resolution, often by denying the claim.

Litigation over property coverage issues could fill volumes, and that is not our intent here. The point of this discussion is that if insurers and their marketing and claims representatives are going to avoid disputes with their own insureds over coverage, they have to be extremely careful in their analysis of the claim. Virtually every one of these situations—except where courts may have altered an interpretation—could be resolved with a thorough investigation of coverage, that first step of adjusting. Far too many like to move to the third step, negotiation or resolution, often by denial. That's wrong, It is simply unethical practice and generally also malpractice.

Defaults and Statute of Limitation Errors

The danger associated with a statute of limitations is that an adjuster's actions easily can lead to an allegation of estoppel. This is often termed *lulling*. When an adjuster is unaware of an approaching statute, he may deal with someone as if there were all the time in the world to resolve the claim. If the person relies upon this impression and the statute runs on their claim, estopple may toll (set aside) the statute.

One method to combat such problems is to establish and enforce rules that applicable statutes and dates be identified and noted on the file jacket. Similar electronic notations can be made in computerized claim systems. When the reminder date approaches, notice should be sent to the party(s) involved that a statute of limitations date is approaching. If the claim is owed, an offer may be made with the maximum time limit for consideration the statute expiration date or a few days prior to it.   This permits the adjuster to follow up verbally on whether the party wishes to settle, plans to abandon the claim, or has retained counsel to file a lawsuit before the statute date expires.

Stay Out of Trouble

Establish and enforce rules that applicable statutes and dates be identified and noted on the file jacket. Similar electronic notations can be made in computerized claim systems.

In California, for example, the state Unfair Claims Settlement Practices Act specifies that insurers must notify unrepresented claimants with whom they are negotiating that a statute soon will expire. Since the state's bodily injury statute is only one year, this is an appropriate rule.

It may be advantageous to the insurer to temporarily waive an approaching statute if negotiations on an expensive claim are underway and expected to be successful. A thirty- or sixty-day extension often can help bring a bogged-down negotiation to fruition without the expense of litigation.

Excess Liability

When a liability insurer fails to protect the interests of its insured within the policy limits, it can be exposed to allegations of bad faith. Exactly what this means in terms of an E&O claim, however, can be confusing; it depends entirely on the situation. When an individual is involved in a serious accident and her coverage is insufficient for all the claims, there is little danger of a bad faith claim as long as the insurer investigates, defends, and otherwise acts with good intentions toward the insured to settle on her behalf.

However, a variety of missteps can result in a bad faith claim. Additionally, the bases for such claims differ from state to state. What is bad faith in one state may not be in another. Many textbooks outline such circumstances by state. Nevertheless, a few simple rules may help to keep adjusters out of trouble:

1. If there is a coverage issue, discover it quickly and place the insured on notice of it immediately. Then attempt to resolve it if possible. If it cannot be resolved, or if coverage is not specifically denied, consider the insured a partner in his own defense. If the insurer defends the insured under a reservation of rights, the insured is entitled to hire his own attorney. In California and several other states adopting the so-called *Cumis* Doctrine (based on *San Diego Federal Credit Union v. Cumis Ins. Society Inc.,* 208 Cal. Rptr. 494 [1984]), the defending insurer may be required to pay for separate counsel to represent the insured when there is a potential conflict of interest. An unresolved coverage issue, almost by definition, would be such a conflict. The insured must be kept fully informed of every aspect of the claim.

2. Advise the insured as soon as possible when potential or actual claims against her may ex-

ceed policy limits. This is done through an excess letter. It should suggest that if the insured has any other insurance that may apply to the claim, he should at once notify that insurer to become involved in the claim.

3. Try to find other coverage that may supplement the primary insurer's responsibility.

4. Carefully investigate and evaluate the liability of the insured to third-party claimant(s). Determine whether there is there any offsetting comparative or contributory negligence. Examples include manufacturers of products that might be involved, those responsible for maintaining the premises where the loss occurred, or any other party that helped to cause the loss or created a hazard that contributed to the loss.

5. Be cautious when trying to save a few bucks in the negotiations. If it is a policy limits case, attempt to settle the case for those limits as soon as possible. As noted previously, the insurer's failure to try to get a release of the insured in an excess situation may be considered bad faith. The adjuster must know the case law in applicable jurisdictions.

6. If there are more claims than money, consider paying the policy limits into the court for the court to distribute. Again, some states allow this as a means of settlement while others do not.

7. When there are excess or contributing insurers, the adjuster owes a good faith duty to settle for them as well as for the policyholder.

8. In most states the duty to defend is as great or greater than the duty to settle. The insurer has a duty to be in control of the litigation and must

work closely with defense counsel and the insured in a tripartite relationship.

Million dollar verdicts are still somewhat rare. What the public does not always hear is the outcome of the appeals of such verdicts. Even when a jury awards an astronomical verdict against an insured with limited coverage, the duty of the insurer may not be over until the very last appeal is heard and the final judgments become due.

Improper Use of Surveillance and Invasion of Privacy

Because of the volume of alleged fraud involving insurance claims, the industry cannot afford to be naïve. It must be nosey when it underwrites a risk, and it must be nosey when it settles a claim. That is part of the good faith requirement of an understanding relationship that builds trust.

The nosey agent or adjuster may seem to be prying, but information *is* his business. Without building the relationship, mutual understanding and trust between the insured and the insurer cannot be achieved. It is when the insurer goes beyond relationship-building in its inquiries that problems can develop.

> **Stay Out of Trouble**
>
> *Without building the relationship, mutual understanding and trust between the insured and the insurer cannot be achieved. Problems result when the insurer goes beyond relationship-building in its inquiries.*

If there is a reason to suspect a breach of trust on the part of the policyholder, the insurer has a duty to investigate, to determine that continued faith and trust in the insured is warranted. However, absent a valid reason to lack faith in the insured, a breach of trust and an invasion of privacy may be unfair. It may even result in allegations of emotional distress.

Disputes over an insurer's investigation often result in litigation. In the Washington case of *Tran v. State Farm Fire & Cas. Co.*, 961 P.2d 358 (1998), the issue was the insured's failure to cooperate. The insured claimed a theft loss but refused to provide financial records to the insurer. The insurer, therefore, denied the claim for lack of cooperation and was sued by the insured. The case went to the state supreme court, which ruled that the insurer had been prejudiced by the insured's failure to provide the requested information, as the insurer had the right under the policy to examine and audit the insured's records. The court also ruled that the insurer had a legitimate reason for broadening its investigation to include a motive for fraud after the insured failed to document his claim or meet with the insurer's representatives.

To what extent may an insurer investigate? The ISO personal auto policy conditions require a person seeking coverage (under medical payments or uninsured motorists coverages, for example) to "submit, as often as we reasonably require: To physical exams by physicians we select...." For life insurance, an underwriting physical examination is often conducted. Of course, such exams must be pertinent. If a person claims a broken arm, the insurer cannot test the person for anything else. If, on the other hand, the exam is for life insurance, the insurer may examine for any condition that might prove life-threatening.

As long as the scope of any insurer's investigation is pertinent to the claim or the coverage, it is ethical. It is only when such an examination goes beyond that limitation that it becomes invasive and unfair.

Defamation, Slander, and Discrimination

While several types of general or employment liability policies include coverage for personal injury offenses ranging from libel, slander, defamation, and false imprisonment to harassment and discrimination, insurers also can fall victim to these perils. Individual adjusters have been sued for slander because of their methods. An adjuster, for instance, might be investigating a possibly fraudulent injury claim and contact the claimant's neighbors. A statement such as, "I'm conducting an insurance fraud investigation against your neighbor and wonder if you might be able to answer some questions for me?" is bound to get back to the neighbor and her attorney. *Bingo!* She just hit the jackpot!

Insurers face potential claims for defamation and other personal injuries in many situations. In the Texas case of *St. Paul Surplus Lines v. Dal-Worth Tank Co., Inc.,* 974 S.W.2d 51 (1998), for example, the insurer's refusal to pay a claim allegedly resulted in a decline of the insured's credit reputation. In a Florida case, *Time Ins. Co. v. Burger,* 712 So.2d 389 (1998), the insurer's delay in paying the insured's medical bills, with subsequent dunning from the provider, allegedly caused the insured emotional distress. A jury awarded him $50,000 plus $1 million in punitive damages for violation of the state's bad faith statute.

Rate discrimination cases arising out of economic factors, age, sex, or other underwriting considerations are, as noted in earlier chapters, not uncommon. Typical of such actions was *Nationwide Mutl. Ins. Co. v. Cisneros*, 52 F.3d 1351 (6th Cir. 1995), in which the U.S. Dept. of Housing & Urban Development (HUD) alleged illegal redlining by the property and casualty insurance industry under the Fair Housing Act.

Being Aware

The problem in many insurance-related companies is that the people normally involved in situations in which an error can result in a claim are seemingly unaware of their exposures. It is not only the key operatives who can create a situation leading to a malpractice claim. Problems arising from time-sensitive matters, such as situations in which payment must be made within a certain number of days, can result from clerical actions as well. A document may be placed with the wrong file, or the person in charge of the file may be out sick, and the lawsuit may not be called to a supervisory person's attention. Date-stamping incoming mail and documents and preserving the envelopes as proof of when they were mailed can be vitally important steps when managing the E&O risk.

Educating staff about E&O claims is an ongoing necessity. New exposures are constantly arising. Old ones continue. The computer age brings endless new exposures, such as the vulnerability of claim data and file information to hackers. Unless a firm is committed to saving itself a lot of trouble, E&O claims will eat away at both that firm's time and money. A serious lawsuit can consume hundreds of hours of employee and executive time. The defense is expensive, and any settlements costly. But like any risk, those losses can be controlled.

Thought Provokers

1. What is the difference between an agent's or broker's legal obligations to inquire into her customer's risk needs—beyond the immediately requested coverage—and any ethical duty to do so?

2. Determine whether spoliation of evidence is an actionable tort in the jurisdiction(s) in which you do business.

3. Even when an insurance policy reserves the contractual right to "repair or replace the damaged or stolen property" to the insurer, why might it be unwise for an insurance company adjuster to authorize repairs on behalf of the insured?

4. How might misinterpreting a coverage issue lead to an allegation of waiver and estoppel in the following situations?

   a. The insured is sued for injuries resulting from an auto accident while driving his employer's uninsured truck.

   b. The insured is sued for vandalism damages allegedly caused by his teenaged son while joy riding with the neighbor's son in the neighbor's car.

Thought Provokers

5. A windstorm damages an insured's home. The insureds were separated, and a few weeks after the storm their divorce was finalized. There are three mortgages on the dwelling, and many of the contents were damaged or destroyed in the storm. There is a $500 deductible. Many items are subject to sublimits. How can you determine the insurable interests in this claim?

6. What are some ways to prevent problems arising out of statutes of limitations and defaults on lawsuits?

Chapter 9

Ethics and Professionalism

"...[V]iolations of ethical standards are rampant in all professions. We must therefore study our profession and its practices carefully. Right behavior comes through knowledge. Self-interest easily leads us astray."

David Warren, CPCU
CPCU Risk Management Quarterly

As observed throughout this book, ethics in the insurance industry is a very complex subject but one that, if mastered, can greatly enhance both our customers' and our own lives. It also can enhance our profitability and protect us from accusations of malpractice. Within the industry and within individual insurance-related firms, ethics must not be only a top-down commitment toward the paying customer and all of society but also a personal ethical commitment by each individual.

Do You Agree?

Insurance, in many ways, must be part of society's conscience. When bad risks are underwritten, bad results are bound to occur. When insurers shortcut services such as claim investigation, fraud and apathy are the result.

Insurance, in many ways, must be part of society's conscience. When bad risks are underwritten, bad results are bound to occur. When insurers shortcut services such as claim investigation, fraud and apathy are the result.

In a 1981 *Forbes* article, "Ethic Chic," business guru Peter Drucker wrote, "There is only one ethics, one set of rules of morality, one code—that of individual behavior in which the same rules apply to everyone alike." Yet ethics must be much more than morality or sets of rules. Ethics involve individual behavior. Can all ethics be universal? Do we universally agree on what might be considered ethically moral? We also must recognize that there are institutional ethics, societal ethics, even corporate ethics. Do these differ from individual ethics? What seems right and moral for one person may seem entirely wrong for someone else.

The Desire to be Professional

A Higher Duty

Even the slightest breach of the legal duty owed by a professional exposes her to an allegation of malpractice. If we in the vast arena of insurance intend to be professionals, then we must gear ourselves to perform above the normal standard.

One fact gleaned from our analysis of insurance and claim ethics in the twenty-first century is that ethics are closely tied to professionalism. All persons have certain ethical standards—good or bad—but the ethics of any person who is a professional must be far above the standard. While insurance is not a true profession in the same sense as medicine, law, and other recognized professions, it is a professional vocation. The individuals within the field can be—perhaps *should* be—professionals. What that translates to is a matter of both legal and ethical duty. The legal duty owed by any professional is much higher than for a nonprofessional. Even the slightest breach of that duty exposes a professional to an allegation of malpractice. If we in the vast arena of insurance intend to be professionals, then we must gear our ethics to perform above the normal standard.

The Prognosis for Professional Liability

Practitioners in insurance-related vocations have been fortunate to avoid many of the pitfalls that burden other professions. As noted previously in several legal citations, the courts have carefully analyzed each situation coming before it and imposed a relatively modest standard of care upon our industry. Neither the courts nor governmental agencies have been that soft on the medical, legal, engineering, or accounting professions. This may be because any malpractice in those fields can be life threatening, if not already fatal. However, as we push toward professionalism we can anticipate that the glare of the professional liability spotlight will increase. We will not be able to escape pitfalls as easily as in the past.

How, then, can we address this increasingly dangerous professional liability prognosis? One way is through improvement of our personal, corporate, and institutional ethics.

The Ethics of Accuracy

It takes time and effort to produce accurate information, and information is perhaps the most important factor in insurance ethics.

Without correct information, not one step in the insurance process can be taken without the possibility of error; neither party can proceed with the objective of complete faith and fair dealing.

How we acquire information and verify its correctness has changed over the last three decades. Today we rely on computer data banks and other electronic information sources. While one might argue that this shifts the ethical burden for accuracy from the insurance practitioner to the producer of the data, what it actually does is increase the practitioner's ethical duty to verify that the information in the data bank is accurate. If we are lazy and accept computerized data as sacrosanct without verification, errors and omissions will occur.

Verifying Data

If we are lazy and accept computerized data as sacrosanct without verification, errors and omissions will occur.

Information comes to us in many forms. Often the best source of good information is derived from the personal relationship between the parties involved in the transaction. If we define faith as requiring trust and belief based largely upon a caring and understanding relationship, then we must investigate in order to understand.

Building Trust not Easy

How can we build an understanding relationship of trust in the brief encounters of an insurance transaction? Ultimately, insurance is not just a financial product; it is a matter of personal and individual need.

How can we build an understanding relationship of trust in the brief encounters of an insurance transaction? The only possible way is to focus on the accuracy of the information and its applicability to the circumstances. We must exercise every aspect of human relations, for ultimately insurance is not just a financial product; it is a matter of personal and individual need.

The Ethics of Listening

If the information needed to build the required full faith or utmost good faith relationship ultimately must come from a personal relationship with the other parties, we must be keenly attuned to those persons in our contacts. We must listen to the other party and hear what he really is telling us.

Listen and Hear

We must listen to the other party and hear what he really is telling us.

There is a difference between listening and hearing. Recent human behavior studies have shown that women "listen" with both halves of their brain, while men only use half of their brain to listen. Perhaps this is why men, more than women, hear those three little words ("but you said...") more often than women.

This physiological phenomenon may be due to evolution; women need to listen for the sounds of their children more than men do. They are more attuned to the social aspects of life. Perhaps this is why insurance marketing and claim adjusting are shifting from predominantly masculine to feminine vocations.

Nevertheless, for both men and women in the insurance vocation, the need to listen is vital. The need to hear what is said and also to hear what may not be said, to read the innuendo, is crucial in the gathering of accurate information. It comes not only with use of our ears but also with the use of our minds, our learning, and our experiences.

A couple of decades ago several prominent business schools devised a system called Management by Objective (MBO). Like many business systems, this one was based on a universal truth: If you have a goal, it is much easier to be successful.

But all the MBAs with their MBOs may have missed a crucial point. Precise systems based on formulas and processes seldom achieve what the entity really needs to achieve because there are too many variables. The tried and true processes that develop over time and remain entrenched are often the best systems. *Maybe* there is a valid reason that it has always been done that way! *Perhaps* it is not only the right way and the best way—it also may be the most ethical way. Deciding whether it is or not remains the technical, perhaps ethical, dilemma!

Business critic and author Tom Peters came up with another management solution. It was called "Management by Wandering Around." It required going out to meet with the customers and the employees to discover what they had to say about the business or the product or the service. What would the customers suggest the company do differently? What was their need? What did the employees who were on the line dealing with these customers suggest? What innovations did they have to offer? It all boiled down to listening.

Entire industries sometimes come close to failure because they forget to understand what business they are in. Businesses that operate on the basis of "here is my product—take it or leave it" may fail because they do not listen to the customer. Individual railroads often ran into financial difficulty and failure because they thought they were in the railroad business. The survivors knew better. They were in the transportation business. To be fair, the railroads did have many problems, including rate regulation. But not all the regulation, it turns out, was bad. It provided a certain degree of protection. The same is true of insurance regulation. It often enhances the industry.

> **Our Business Is Risk**
>
> *We must remember that we are not in the insurance business. Our business is risk. Our business is loss. Whether we approach that business from the marketing or the claims end, we must never forget that our duty is to help customers with the management of that risk or loss.*

We must remember that we are *not* in the insurance business. Our business is risk. Our business is loss. Whether we approach that business from the marketing or the claims end, we must never forget that our duty is to help customers with the management of that risk or loss. Even though not all the risk is insurable nor all the loss claimable, we cannot approach our customers on a take-it or leave-it basis. As professionals we must listen to that customer, help him to diagnose his risk or loss problem, consider options and choices, and carefully analyze all the information in order to come up with the best solution.

The Ethics of Learning

In the last three decades there have been many changes in the insurance field. My first teaching experience was coaching new adjusters to pass the state adjuster's license exam. It was a tough examination with a high failure rate. Teaching those new adjusters the ins and outs of coverage was one of the hardest jobs I had ever undertaken. There seemed to be little commitment by some of those students to study what they considered to be superfluous coverage information; the exam covered all lines of insurance, and they dealt only in casualty coverages.

A while later I began to teach the 240-hour required property-casualty state agents licensing course. Here was a different type of student. Many class members were Cuban refugees who spoke little or no English. The state then allowed them to take the exam in Spanish.

These men and women—both young and old—never missed a class. The non-English-speaking students recorded the lectures to be translated later by family members. All were dedicated students, eager to make a success of their new freedoms in America. For several years these students scored higher on the state exam than most of the students who had taken the same courses at state universities. While some of them had been insurance agents or underwriters in Cuba, they were still at a disadvantage, but they were committed. They did not see some of the more remote coverages as superfluous.

At that time insurance companies and support institutions such as the American Institute for CPCU and the College of Life Underwriters offered complex university-graduate level educational programs. Insurers also operated their own schools.

In the 1970s, however, something began to change. At first it was subtle—only a name change. Education departments in insurance-related organizations across the nation became training units. Insurance vocations were open to virtually anyone, regardless of academic background.

The new employees often were ill equipped for the typical insurance education classroom where, as in universities, the regimen was lecture and written essay examinations. Many employees were less proficient in writing skills than had previously been the case.

Subtle changes became more overt. True/false and multiple-choice examinations began to replace the essay tests. Recorded statements replaced hand-written statements. New computerized tools became available that undertook complicated calculations and decision-making. *Education* had taught students *why* something was so; *training*, on the other hand, was intended to teach a student *how* to do something. There is a difference. Knowing why something is done directly affects the ability of students to become true professionals.

A profession requires both general and specific knowledge. No one can become a surgeon without many years of classroom education and study. One doesn't just train to be a surgeon—physicians must learn

> **Education versus Training**
>
> *Education* had taught students *why* something was so; *training*, on the other hand, was intended to teach a student *how* to do something. There is a difference. Knowing why something is done directly affects the ability of students to become true professionals.

why surgery is done, where it is done, when it is done, on whom it is done, and what must be done long before learning how to do it!

If the insurance industry is to be a true profession, it must recommit itself to real programs of education. Unless and until such a commitment is made by the industry, there will be little reason for young people to want to dedicate their lives to a career in insurance. What does that forecast for the future of the industry?

A new type of academic degree may be needed, such as a bachelor or master of risk science. The degree would combine the arts and sciences, especially areas of communication, with a general education background. It could include both academic and hands-on training. This degree should encompass the entire spectrum of life. Why? Because that is what the insurance profession encompasses.

The Ethics of Responsibility

When the circumstances call for us to be in charge, we must be prepared to do whatever is required. When the circumstances only call for us to be in control, however, we must understand the role and be prepared to act in that capacity. To misunderstand these separate duties is to set ourselves up for an ethical and professional breach.

Separate Duties

To misunderstand the separate duties of being in charge and being in control is to set ourselves up for an ethical and professional breach.

We encounter breaches of the separate duties frequently. An example is the contract storm adjuster who, when he got into a legal dispute over repairs he had authorized, announced in his deposition that he, as an adjuster, was "in charge of the case" and that he had "authority to proceed as I see best." He had forgotten that it was the insured who had to be in charge of the loss; he was only supposed to be in control of the claim!

There are, however, those who exercise their responsibilities with professionalism. They are natural born leaders. They are few in number. Those who are given leadership responsibility must be emotionally and professionally prepared to perform and encourage others. The other type are those

There Are Professionals

There are, however, those who exercise their responsibilities with professionalism.

who want to be in charge but are not good leaders or lack the authority and professionalism to lead. These are the power hungry who may rise to a supervisory level where they are inefficient and ineffective. They make poor leaders, and those both above and below them suffer as a result. Unfortunately there are many of these types within the insurance industry who assert their authority in unprofessional ways.

Recognizing the Customer

At times the biggest problem for some is recognizing his customer. It often is unclear in the insurance world who the client or principal really is, for there are many contractual relationships that must be considered along with the basic insured-insurer policy contract. The insurance industry's customers are not only the ones who purchase the insurance—the policyholder. Users of the coverage also are customers.

Tom Peters, in an analysis of corporate successes, best explained this by asking, "Who is CNN's customer?" Individuals with cable television undoubtedly watch many all-news cable channels. Are viewers of those stations' customers? Sure they are! The programs are broadcast for viewer patronage. Sponsors and advertisers aim their messages at viewers. Do they bill viewers regularly for their programs? No. Cable companies are the ones that pay for transmitting those channels, along with the movies, sports, and the specialty cable channels. So the viewers are not really CNN's customers, the cable company is. But the viewers are the users, the parties for whom CNN's product is intended.

The same is true in insurance. In mandatory auto liability states every vehicle owner is required by law to purchase liability insurance. That insured is the customer, but he is not the party who directly benefits from the product (except in no-fault states). The users are those to whom the insured becomes liable.

Agents and brokers arrange for purchase of workers compensation insurance, which is required by law in most states of most employers. The employer-insured is the customer, but the employer is not the direct beneficiary of the coverage; purchase of the coverage only places the employer in compliance with the law. The users of the coverage are that employer's injured employees. Are they not the true customers of the service provided?

Why do commercial entities hire employees? They hire and train employees in order to get the work done in order to make a profit for the business or accomplish the role of the institution. The employer who is in control of his employees knows that they are valuable; their injuries disrupt the flow of work and revenue. Employers fix broken equipment quickly to get it back into service. Likewise, the policy-holder-customer wants to get injured employees back to work as quickly as possible. By treating injured employees as if they were the real customers, the insurer in effect benefits the paying customer.

Why, then, do so many insurers and their claim representatives treat third-party claimants and injured employees as if they were an enemy? Why do so many third-party claimants and employees seek attorneys to represent them in their claims against the insurer? Could it be that insurers have been treating these product users as if the insurer were in charge instead of the injured or damaged party?

"Does a professional insurance company claims representative have an ethical responsibility to recommend to a claimant that he or she obtain legal representation prior to settling the claim?" This question was asked by Professor Peter R. Kensicki of Eastern Kentucky University, a member of the CPCU Society Ethics Committee, in an October 2000 column in *National Underwriter*. Answers were re-ported in the February 19, 2001, issue. The responses covered a broad spectrum but generally were "no." Said one adjuster, "If the claims representative is truly a professional and proficient in the craft, rarely is it necessary to ever require a third-party [representative] to bring the matter to a fair resolution." An agent replied that "as an agent, I believe that I work for the consumer. I should be the one that offers that advice." Perhaps the agent missed one point while hitting another. Yes, a third-party claimant *is* the consumer, but the agent is not in a position to be in control of that consumer, only his own client.

An insurer's attorney offered some estimates of third-party repre-sentation, noting that "slightly over 50 percent" of all claims have attorney involvement and that 80 percent of those are settled without a lawsuit. Only 2 percent of litigated files actually go to trial. Kensicki summarizes that attorney's response as "with lawyers so prevalent in the system, withholding a recommendation to seek legal counsel is not contributing to or taking advantage of an unusual situation or knowingly permitting a claimant to proceed at a disadvantage." The reality is that if the reputation of the insurance industry were really one

Loss versus Claim
Often the loss is greater than the claim, just as the duty to defend may be greater than the duty to pay.

of full faith and fair dealing, third-party attorney representation would decline.

Insurers and their representatives have an ethical duty to help those customers—both policyholders and policy users—to understand any loss that may occur but to control only the resulting claim. Often the loss is greater than the claim, just as the duty to defend may be greater than the duty to pay. This responsibility seldom puts the insurer or its representatives in charge of the loss. Each party must understand where his responsibility lies.

Personal Integrity

We are each different. Some of us are tall, some short. Some fat, some thin. We are black, white, Hispanic, Native American, Asian, or some other race or ethnicity. With all the differences, how can we ever come to understand the concept of integrity as it applies to ethics?

Is Peter Drucker correct that the same rules apply to everyone? Is there some sort of corporate or national integrity? Does only one set of moral rules exist for all?

We defined integrity in the introduction as a wholeness. Perhaps, despite all the diversity, there is a common ethical element among us. If so, what is it, and how does it relate to professionalism in insurance matters? Philosophers may speak of some sort of natural law, an inborn knowledge of right and wrong. This we might call morals. We instinctively know that it is wrong to kill or steal or lie, yet for each of these rules there are many morally acceptable—perhaps necessary—exceptions.

There is also the law of nature, biologists tell us. Perhaps there is integrity in all of nature: the wholeness of our need for survival.

Like humans, birds have a pecking order. It is not necessarily by size. The wren and the titmouse will share the feeder, but if machine-gun Kelly, the redheaded woodpecker, comes to feed, the other birds wait patiently in the branch for him to finish. There seems to be within humans a similar understanding of place. That, too, is part of integrity: our inward natural conception of a role we each play in society. We submit to authority. We share responsibilities of home and job with family and co-workers. We are cautious of dangers and mourn disaster. We protect our children and loved ones. As in humans, there is an ethic that all life understands.

In another sense, however, integrity is individualized and personal. There are many who believe that behavior is primarily influenced by genes. Others believe that environment is the key to behavior. Bad kids often come from bad neighborhoods, but so do many successful people; just as many bad folks come from good neighborhoods. Our associations do not necessarily determine our behavior. We are each different.

> **Universal and Personal**
>
> *There is an ethic that all life understands. In another sense, however, integrity is individualized and personal.*

The role of integrity in ethics must be a combination of societal and personal morality. It must be much more than the Golden Rule. As Rev. Thomas H. Conley of Atlanta recently pointed out, "Do unto others as you would have them do unto you" is contingent on one's own standard. Do we really want people to treat us the way we might treat someone else? Perhaps our desire is for a standard of treatment much higher than *that*!

Morality implies many things: virtue, knowing right from wrong, doing right, and being of a quality character. It implies behavior and how one conducts himself. It requires truthfulness and constant honesty.

Even though we have said much about the need for top-down corporate ethics within the insurance industry, where the objective of ethics is a matter of constant motivation from the CEO to the lowest clerk, perhaps George Bernard Shaw said it best in *The Irrational Knot* (1905), "Money is indeed the most important thing in the world; and all sound and successful personal and national morality should have this fact for its basis."

Money must motivate what commercial entities do. If a government lacks funds, it cannot fully serve the citizens. If a corporation is unprofitable the stockholders are losers. Employees will be laid off, maintenance will be deferred with a possible increase in employee injuries, stress will be universal, and failure will be possible. Money concerns must motivate that entity.

For individuals, money also may be a motivating factor. As an ethical and moral minimum we must provide for our families and ourselves the basic twenty-first century necessities of life: food, shelter, transportation, education, employment, and financial security. All that takes money. It may be unethical for us not to provide these things for our families and ourselves, for then we become a burden to both society and ourselves. Herein lies the key to integrity and moral behavior: A man who acts unethically in his professional vocation places at risk his—and his employer's—financial resources. This is just as unethical as the man who abandons his family and fails to provide the necessary support. Integrity is wholeness; it applies to the job, the family, the home, and the community. It does not start or stop at the office door.

The Ideal of Altruistic Attitude and Behavior

Altruism could be defined as concern for the welfare of others over concerns for self. It has nothing to do with law, but it may have much to do with codes of honor. It is a key factor separating professionals from nonprofessionals. The professional plumber may get out of his bed to help a customer whose pipe has burst not only because he can charge more for a nighttime visit but because he really wants to help that customer.

The physician who works long hours in the hospital emergency room, the attorney who sits up late at night preparing his case for trial, the clergy person who visits her parishioner when it is inconvenient, the accountant who spends hours reviewing her client's figures in an attempt to find additional resources—each does what she does not because it pays a bit more but because she has the best interests of the customer, the client, the patient, the parishioner, at heart.

Because insurance deals with the risk of loss, opportunities for altruistic behavior abound in our professional vocation. It is shown in how we deal with the potential for loss—helping customers identify and reduce sources of loss—and with how we deal with those who have suffered a loss, whether or not they are our direct customer. It is the act of going beyond what the contract requires. Obviously, we must be careful not to do something that jeopardizes the contractual agreement. But, if we are professional, our ethical standard must take us beyond the contract to *be there*, to put ourselves out for the sake of the other party, to be empathetic with the victim of loss.

Altruism Required

After Hurricane Andrew, adjusters knew where the companies were headquartered, so they often were able to advise victims who were not even their policyholders where to go for help. They were prepared. That, too, was part of the altruism required of the industry and its people.

Perhaps this is most evident in a catastrophe. Hundreds of men and women around the nation have made themselves available for immediate call-up for cat duty after disasters. These people are paid well, and many work twenty, even twenty-four-hour, days. They have learned to deal not only with the claim—which is the concern of their employers—but also with the loss.

After Hurricane Andrew, many victims had no idea how to contact their insurers. When adjusters arrived in the neighborhood these homeless refugees descended upon them and begged for help. The adjusters knew where the companies were headquartered, so they often were able to advise the victims who were not even their policyholders where to go for help. The insurers responded faster than governmental agencies responsible for such disaster assistance. They were prepared. That, too, was part of the altruism required of the industry and its people.

Role of Professional Organizations and the State

In Chapter 2 we discussed the requirements that make a vocation a true profession. They included not only educational and licensing factors, but the role of an organization of professional peers to control admittance to the profession. The state bar associations for attorneys are perhaps the best example of this. If you do not have a law degree, you cannot sit for the bar examination; if you do not pass the bar exam, you cannot be admitted to practice law before the courts; if you act unethically, you can be disbarred and booted out of the profession.

In each true profession the association or other organization has a career life-and- death hold over the practitioner. If the applicant does not comply with the entrance requirements, she cannot become a member of the profession. If the organization withdraws support, that person must withdraw from the field. Licensing by the state is only one aspect of this process. In professions, even the state's licensing is subject to the organization's participation and control.

There is no such organization for the insurance industry. There are no academic requirements to enter the field, no organization with life-and-death authority over careers, no industry watchdog. There is some state authority to license and revoke licenses, but this amounts to little more than an examination or continuing education.

Without some sort of nationally recognized insurance organization that sets academic requirements for those entering the field, that requires matriculation, that provides mentoring and continuing education, that works closely with the state on licensing procedures, and that maintains a financial life-and-death hold over the membership in both the quality of performance and ethical standards, no vocation can be a true profession.

There are subprofessions within the industry, such as the field of actuarial science through actuarial societies. Actuarial fellowship designations place them among the most prestigious professionals in the insurance industry. Similar steps toward true professionalism are present in other financial services organizations such as the CPCU (Chartered Property & Casualty Underwriter) Society and the Chartered Life Underwriter program. Other organizations are dedicated to professionalism and continuing education, such as the National Association of Insurance Women (International) and the Registered Professional Adjusters associations. Such educational organizations offer over seventy academic designations upon completion of the required curriculum.

Unfortunately, many state and local insurance organizations do little to further professionalism. The primary purpose of many of them is social.

The role of the state in insurance is often more a regulatory requirement than professional adherence. Licensing may be viewed as a revenue-raiser as much as it is seen as monitoring qualified professionals. There often are few, if any, prerequisites for licensing other than affirming citizenship, passing the test, and paying the fee.

States, however, can become involved in enforcing insurance codes, including the Unfair Claims Settlement Practices Act. Emphasis is often on political consumerism; state regulators often take the part of the citizen who feels she has been unfairly treated by the insurer— sometimes without carefully analyzing the facts.

The regulator's role is focused primarily on rate regulation, solvency, and enforcement. In some states the regulators review claim files for the timeliness and accuracy of payments, levying heavy fines—into the hundreds of thousands of dollars—on insurers or adjusters who are not in compliance with the laws. This relates primarily to health or workers compensation claims, but also can involve other types of coverage. Procrastination on the payment of a claim is perhaps the greatest sin an insurer can commit.

A common phrase in contracts is that "time is of the essence." It means that undue delay may allow changes in the conditions on which the contract is based and make it invalid. The slightest whiff of delay in settling claims will alarm the regulator, irritate the claimant or insured, and crystallize in an accusation of unethical behavior on the persons who caused the delay.

> **Do You Agree?**
>
> *Procrastination on the payment of a claim is perhaps the greatest sin an insurer can commit.*

Insurance Ethics in the Information Age

A number of factors contribute to ethical behavior within the insurance industry. Most involve personal relationships, the flow of information within the insurance organization itself, and the relationship between the industry and state regulators.

With the advent of the Information Age, personal relationships have diminished. People can purchase insurance online without human involvement by the insurer. Likewise, computers can handle many claims. It's quick and efficient, but, as we noted, it can contribute to the public's poor attitude toward the insurance industry. That attitude is reflected in the amount of alleged fraud that occurs, but it also is reflected in jury response to insurance cases.

This is similar to banks that have encouraged customers to use automatic teller machines by charging a fee when a teller is used. Many banks have discovered that people want personal attention.

E-business undoubtedly is here to stay. Predictions are that we will not only transact banking but will make most purchases by computer. Already some grocery stores allow shoppers to check themselves out with a bar-code reader and a debit card. According to an article in *National Underwriter* in February 2001, both insurers and engineers are predicting that machines will report malfunctions and claims directly without the owner or insured having to call in a loss. Auto to satellite communication systems already have the ability to trigger a damage alarm at the manufacturer's location if the vehicle's electronic system detects an impact. The system can pinpoint an auto's location anywhere in the country and report it to the police in that locality. Anti-auto-theft systems also can utilize satellite systems to track stolen vehicles.

When our washing machine can report a leak to the plumber even when we don't know about it and the car can be programmed to immediately notify the insurer of a theft or collision, we can anticipate ever less personal contact. But if personal contact is necessary to gain the understanding that permits the creation of faith, and if good faith is still a basic requirement of the insurance relationship, then how will this be possible? Perhaps rules for futuristic insurance relationships are needed:

1. Computers, satellite systems, and automation are very useful tools, but they still are only tools.

2. The insurance industry is *not* in the insurance business; it is in the business of risk and the business of loss. It is in the peace-of-mind and the financial stability business. It must use electronic tools to conduct transactions, but human contact must remain in the production of the information involved in the risk and loss, for those are human factors as well as mechanical factors.

3. Computer data must be verified. To assume that information transmitted by a computerized data system is sacrosanct is a sure path to professional malpractice.

4. We always must know who is supposed to be in charge, who needs to be in control, and who must respond to those two factors.

5. Data going into a system must be accurate. The old expression, "garbage in, garbage out," is crucially true.

6. Loss data is used for a variety of claim, premium, and actuarial purposes. Insurer reports to insureds should be presented in clear language and logical order, with specific reference to the policy language or claims when appropriate.

7. Where transactions are made entirely by telephone or computer, either electronic or postal confirmation should be made within a short time span.

8. Electronic claim payments, such as direct deposit of periodic payments or use of a debit card in a catastrophe claim, also should require electronic or postal confirmation within twenty-four hours.

9. Electronic negotiation of third-party claims should provide electronic or postal confirmation of any demand or offer within twenty-four hours in the event that settlement is not achieved. Settlement agreements and electronically produced releases also should be confirmed within twenty-four hours to all involved parties.

10. Privacy and security of data is paramount.

A Personal Code of Ethics

For anyone in the insurance industry who seeks to be considered a professional, a personal code of ethics is a basic requirement. It should be personal—specific to the tasks undertaken and the roles played within the overall insurance process. The personal ethics of insurance marketers by definition would differ from those of claim adjusters or attorneys. Agent or broker codes also would differ.

Regardless of the individual area of the industry served, however, there are common elements that should be included in any personal code of ethics. These include factors such as

> **Personal Code Necessary**
>
> *For anyone in the insurance industry who seeks to be considered a professional, a personal code of ethics is a basic requirement. It should be personal—specific to the tasks undertaken and the roles played within the overall insurance process.*

- considering the customer's or service user's needs above one's own,

- examining not only the covered peril or claim but also the risk and loss,

- protecting the privacy of others,

- being accurate in details used to produce needed information, and

- adhering to the laws and regulations that affect insurance transactions.

There also must be a commitment to professionalism. This must be a part of any ethics code and take the form of an educational standard, continuing academic study, membership in professional organizations, participation in community activities, and integrity toward family and society. Codes of ethics also must include the monetary factor, the rewards of professionalism. An ethics code should, therefore, include a demand that the person achieving professional status be entitled to reap the rewards of that status in both financial compensation and community recognition.

Money Is Important

There must be a commitment to professionalism. Codes of ethics also must include the monetary factor, the rewards of professionalism.

Insurance professionals—even if insurance is not a true profession in and of itself—are not in the business of buying and selling policies and claim settlements as if they were widgets from a factory. The product is not just paper and money, it is peace of mind, assistance with loss, financial strength when needed, and security and protection. Insurance is more than just a financial institution like a bank or investment market. The price of stocks and bonds can fluctuate daily because of market influences; insurance service cannot. It must be based on solid and accurate data, and its premium rating must be fair and adequate at all times. When insurers attempt to operate strictly like other businesses, they risk missing the ethics of their responsibilities to their policyholders.

Thought Provokers

1. Relate the concept of full faith and fair dealing to the specific insurance-related tasks you perform daily in you career.

2. Is an ethical or moral standard solely individualistic or is it universal? In what ways are ethics individual, and in what ways are they universal?

3. What role does the state's insurance regulatory agency play in your particular tasks? Must you be licensed, and, if so, what is required for that license? How do you maintain it? Relate that process to ethics.

4. How has electronic commerce affected your job? Do you see the use of computerized systems as advantageous or disadvantageous to your customers? How would you go about improving customer relations through computerized electronic communications?

5. Write a personal code of ethics for your insurance profession.

References

Bortner, R. Mark, J.D. "Cyberlaundering: Anonymous Digital Cash and Money Laundering." University of Miami Law School, 1996.

Brownlee, Kenneth J. *Casualty, Fire & Marine Investigation Checklists, Fifth Edition.* New York: West Group, 1998.

Brownlee, Kenneth J. "Defending the "Self-Insured" or "Self-Funded" Entity." *Insurance Litigation Reporter* (West) 22, no. 15 (Sept. 2000): 465-486.

Covey, Stephen R. *The Seven Habits of Highly Effective People.* New York: Simon & Schuster, 1989.

Failey, Fred W. "Watch Rob Run." *Trains,* January 2000.

Magarick, Pat, and Kenneth J. Brownlee. *Casualty Insurance Claims.* New York: West Group, 1995.

Markham, James J. *Property Loss Adjusting, Vol. II.* Malvern, Pa.: American Institute for CPCU.

Peter, Dr. Laurence J., and Raymond Hull. *The Peter Principle—Why Things Always Go Wrong.* New York: William Morrow, 1969.

Rowling, J.K. *Harry Potter and the Chamber of Secrets.* New York: Arthur A. Levine Books, 1999.

Russell, Bertrand. *A History of Western Philosophy.* New York: Simon & Schuster, 1945.

Tobias, Andrew. *The Invisible Bankers: Everything the Insurance Industry Never Wanted You to Know.* New York: Linden Press/Simon & Shuster, 1982.

Toffler, Alvin. *Future Shock.* New York: Random House, 1970.

Toffler, Alvin. *The Third Wave.* New York: Wm. Morrow & Co., Inc., 1980.

Warren, David, CPCU. "Understanding Ethics." *CPCU Risk Management Quarterly* (American Institute for CPCU) Vol. II, no. 3 (Sept. 1994).

Warren, Samuel, and Louis Brandeis. "The Right to Privacy." *Harvard Law Review IV* 193 (1890).

Williams, C. Arthur, Jr. "Unfair Rate Discrimination in Property and Liability Insurance." *Insurance, Government & Social Policy,* Illinois: Richard D. Irwin, Inc., 1969.

Index